SOME ASSEMBLY
REQUIRED

BY LEE CHADWICK

M000236710

SOME ASSEMBLY REQUIRED

Copyright © 2004

Lee J. Chadwick

Publisher:

Meridian International Publishing
Atlanta, Georgia

This cookbook is a collection of favorite recipes,
which are not necessarily original recipes.

All rights reserved. No part of this publication may be reproduced
in any form or by any means, electronic or mechanical, including
photocopy and information storage and retrieval systems, without
permission in writing from the publisher.

Copyright Information: L. David Wolfe and Assoc.
Atlanta, Georgia

Library of Congress Number: 2003114233

ISBN: 0-9718186-8-1

Edited, Designed, and Manufactured by Favorite Recipes® Press
An imprint of

FRP

PO Box 305142
Nashville, Tennessee 37230
1-800-358-0560

Art Director: Jim Scott
Project Manager: Susan Larson

Manufactured in the United States of America
First Printing 2004 7,500 copies

DEDICATION

This book is dedicated in spirit and philosophy to my dear mother-in-law, Gertrude Chadwick, a wonderful person but perhaps the world's worst cook. When my husband, Chad, and I were married thirty years ago, we moved immediately to Chicago—1,500 miles away from our families and anyone else we had ever known.

I came from a family of excellent cooks, but I had never been interested in the kitchen. I was a glamour girl and an opinionated eater only. At twenty-one, I had never made my own PBJ or baked a frozen pizza. My husband had been married before—a shocking complication in the dark ages of the 1970s—so we eloped. The consequence of this elopement was no showers, few gifts, limited pots and pans, and no cookbooks! The really great and inspiring side of that is no limitations! No person or author was telling me the "right" way to do *anything*, so I entered the kitchen often and fearlessly.

We had to eat, and we were far too poor to eat out. I merely bought things that looked good to start with and cooked them until they tasted good. I rolled the asparagus back and forth in a little butter in a frying pan because I had only one pot (in which I was boiling the potatoes already). The result was sheer perfection, a great improvement over boiling...a happy accident interpreted as pure genius! My additional inspiration came from the response of my husband (a normally unenthusiastic guy) to a frying chicken slowly roasted for nine hours at 225 degrees while we were at work. He was astonished that you could make a chicken at home without "wings of charcoal." "The meat is so tender it falls off the bone." He was a believer.

Since I did not yet know his mother was an awful cook, his pride and excitement about my newfound "talent" were very energizing and motivating. I moved on to my nine-hour chicken cooked in orange juice with cashew nuts. (Why not?) Next came nine-hour chicken with soy sauce and ginger. This was *brilliantly combined*, I might add, with canned mandarin orange sections successfully chilled for dessert.

"MAYBE I AM A GENIUS," I THOUGHT...THEN CAME THE FATEFUL DAY TWO YEARS LATER...JUST AS I WAS REACHING MY STRIDE. AND REMEMBER, WE WERE ALREADY HOSTING DINNER PARTIES, BUT I STILL DIDN'T OWN A MEASURING CUP! (WE WERE UP TO SIX PLATES, HOWEVER).

I WAS ALREADY GIVING ADVICE—LOTS OF IT—AND ENJOYING A REPUTATION FOR GLOBALLY INFLUENCED CREATIVITY. IN OUR SOCIAL CIRCLE, WE WERE THE ONES WHO OWNED CHOPSTICKS. THEN WE MADE OUR FIRST TRIP "BACK EAST" TO VISIT OVER THANKSGIVING...I WAS SITTING IN THE KITCHEN VISITING WITH MOTHER CHADWICK WHILE SHE WAS GETTING READY TO "MAKE DRESSING" AND START THE TURKEY. SHE PROCEEDED TO OPEN A BAG OF NEWLY PURCHASED WONDER BREAD AND BEGAN TO PUSH ONE UNALTERED SLICE AFTER ANOTHER "AS IS" INTO THE CAVITY OF THE BIRD—NO SALT, NO SPICE, NOTHING! MY BREATHING SLOWED...IF I HAVE EVER HAD A "WATERSHED" EXPERIENCE, ONE IN WHICH YOUR ENTIRE BELIEF SYSTEM IS CLARIFIED IN A FLASH, THIS WAS IT. I HAD, ON MANY OCCASIONS, SEEN MY OWN MOTHER SAUTÉEING SAUSAGE AND APPLES, FILLING THE HOUSE WITH FRAGRANCE, THEN ONIONS AND CELERY, MAKING BROTH FROM THE NECK TO MOISTEN, ETC. THIS WONDER BREAD THING WAS DEFINITELY *NOT DRESSING*! NOW I KNEW, WITHOUT A DOUBT, MY HUSBAND'S OPINION WAS NOT BASED ON MY RECENTLY REVEALED "GIFTS" BUT ON THE FACT THAT HE HAD NEVER EATEN "REAL" FOOD IN HIS LIFE!

FORTUNATELY, MY CONFIDENCE WAS NOT ERODED. I WAS ALREADY SUCCESSFUL IN SPITE OF THE FACT THAT I REALLY DID NOT KNOW HOW TO COOK ANYTHING...YET.

I TELL YOU THIS STORY FOR TWO REASONS:
1. CONFIDENCE IS MORE USEFUL THAN INFORMATION.
2. OTHER PEOPLE'S APPRECIATION OF YOUR EFFORT IS MORE IMPORTANT THAN "TALENT."

YOU CAN SIMPLY ENJOY YOUR LIFE MORE BY PARTAKING OF AND SHARING WONDERFUL FOOD. ONCE YOU VALUE THESE EXPERIENCES, YOU WILL WANT TO EXPAND THE OPPORTUNITIES.

INTRODUCTION
PERSPECTIVE & PHILOSOPHY

This book has been created with the assumption that the reader does not want a culinary education—just dinner, or stylish snacks. So, you will not find a lot of ranting about hormones and antibiotics in meat or irradiation of vegetables or genetic modification of seeds. Find out about these issues elsewhere when you're ready.

More than a cookbook, this is a series of ideas about style and comfort. Both of these are matters of taste. My greatest hope is that after cruising through these pages, you will find your own style emerging from the way you translate and alter my work and the contributions of others. This is a highly personal book because food and fulfillment are very personal matters. Have fun with it...relax...know who your friends are, and seek inspiration in EVERYTHING!

As you enjoy the success you will achieve following the very simple "instructions" and ideas (or recipes), you will no doubt grow more curious about a lot of things, and the grocery store will seem a significantly more interesting place. The rather narrow boundaries for the content herein are designed to truly "underwhelm." Kitchen phobics can look at this book and say out loud, "I can do that!" and they will be right! Just to be safe, we won't even call it cooking, just....assembly!!

You will find this book mysteriously missing most absolutes, because what is GOOD when it comes to food is so subjective. I don't like lentils in soup no matter how skillfully it is prepared, but I love them in the flat crepes common to Indian cuisine. The point is, when YOU like it, only then is it ready to eat, or even worth eating.

There are only a few secrets that you need to know to ensure your success. Whether you are an aspiring cook or a discretionary social eater who just wants to have friends over…let's talk mindset. When I started to teach cooking in the late '70s, I frequently listened to wild stories of how students had selected three, four, even five recipes from a number of sources or books to "try out" at a dinner party for six people. Think about this: could anything be more stressful?

If you do everything exactly right, you still don't know if you will like it! Recipes frequently don't work…literally. How one person measures ingredients, how hot individual ovens are, even the altitude will affect overall results. Imagine intentionally setting up a hungry audience to this marathon of the unexpected! When a new bride or homeowner did not ENJOY this experience, or the food was bad, they were labeled…"can't boil water."

The real learning may come after the fact in the brilliant light of your hindsight…Don't worry. Don't apologize. Don't overreact. Some of your greatest results may come from mistakes—rely on your judgment to determine what is good; if it isn't…it just isn't done yet…maybe. Fear boredom more than failure, and keep something in the pantry or the freezer for the rare occasion when an effort is actually irretrievable. Then forgive yourself and eat! Each experience of making or combining food will bring you a step closer to your "groove"—your food identity. We all have one.

When your own creativity is being released, the process becomes one of freedom more than work. Begin to trust your own instincts so you can live by a different set of rules—yours. Start with something simple that you identify with; then every additional effort you make is a step in the process of mastery.

GOOD COOK—BAD POT

One of the most common reasons for failure among the newly cooking is a bad pot. A pot that does not transfer heat to food in a polite and predictable fashion makes a scrambled egg more difficult than a soufflé. So, it is better to have one good pot than a thousand mediocre ones.

How does one choose a good pot? Well, first, what happens when you use a bad pot (or pan)? For example, when you try to preheat it before you sauté, it will seem to twist itself up and warp from the burner surface. This means that the one 4-inch square patch that still touches will burn everything immediately and the balance of the pan isn't even hot! A five-star chef would throw a pan like this across the kitchen and order a pizza! Good cookware in its wisdom can coach you if you buy wisely—or it can wait in the cupboard plotting against you! Don't you need all the help you can get?

THE GOOD POT—A TOOL TO LOVE

For a beginner, a good pot doesn't even need to be a namebrand pot. Some of the people that I have taught over the years felt their Calphalon or French Copper was too "judgmental"; they felt foolish heating up Spaghetti-O's or ramen noodles in sexy Cuisinaire stainless. Surely cookware of this caliber was designed for trout or truffles! Not so; this is a just a lack of confidence in yourself. Good pots tell no tales and are happy just to be used, and to be useful.

My favorite (after at least twenty sets of different cookware) is my full stainless steel with glass lids and thick aluminum bottoms encased in stainless. They can go in the dishwasher and are pretty enough to serve in—they do not pit, stain, chip, or tarnish. These are pots that demand little and never bully their owners. Simplify your life, and you'll cook more often. Good pots do heat up slowly; don't try to hurry them. Smile while you wait. Enjoy the fact that you will get to know each other better with every use.

KNIVES—NICE TO NASTY

Strangers to the kitchen usually fear sharp knives. They tend to bestow all manner of villainy on what appears to be a weapon. It is, however, a tool. A dull knife is useless—and very dangerous! Don't let anyone talk you into carbon knives; they take an edge very well, yes, but they are not worth the effort. There are many excellent low-maintenance alternatives that can go directly into the dishwasher. My friend Woody travels with her Cutco knives, and she doesn't really cook! Slicing bread or tomatoes? Knives should be serrated, or have an uneven edge, or be "toothed." A six- or eight-inch "chef's" knife allows you to cut with your fingers out of the way because the part of the blade nearest the handle is wider than the tip, so you can chop celery, onions, or potatoes by pressing down instead of slicing. This is also faster and requires less effort. Excellent knives are not so expensive anymore, so buy yourself a set or a few random pieces until you sense affection emerging for a type. When you start saying "my" knife instead of "a" knife, you are almost there. Remember: Most cuts result from slipping when a dull knife skids off the intended surface...and into you. A sharp knife glides knowingly where you intend it to. After living with bad knives, good knives really do seem psychic!

So, you say...I have a knife, and I have a pot now...How do I get started?

Why not try the Yummy Mushroom Bruschetta when you have a friend over to watch a movie? It is a big improvement over microwave popcorn. With good chardonnay, it could make you weep! The next time you make it, pair it with a mug of modified Campbell's Tomato "Bisque," and it's a meal!

What makes something "good" really successful is a concept I call "natural affinity." Grilled cheese and chili have it; sage and chicken have it, too. Ripe tomatoes and even a little salt. When one food makes a companion food or flavor more enjoyable, that is natural affinity.

Examples:

Black pepper Brie and grape tomatoes • Cranberries and walnuts • Apricots and curry
Fish and fennel • Shrimp and cocktail sauce • Stilton and apple slices

SNACKS, SAVORIES AND SPECIALTY DRINKS

This chapter is the most influential in terms of time-saving "new view" entertaining. I recommend you start by meeting at your house for "a drink and a nibble" before going somewhere ELSE for dinner. A few reasons: (1) You then exit the restaurant and go to your respective homes; no one is still at your house at 2:00 a.m.; (2) You are no longer starving, so you order with far more restraint; (3) You have hosted folks at your home and served something wonderful, so you have lessened your fears or dread of exhaustion without "taking on a dinner party"...yet.

AND MOST IMPORTANTLY, you have spent time with people you enjoy for no other reason than just that. These successes are good practice for full-scale entertaining if you ever choose to do it, or just a really easy relationship rescue. An expanded next-effort version still not called "dinner" is my favorite way to entertain. Three, four, or five items you make, a special coordinated cocktail and matched beer or wine, stylishly presented with purchased items but no dessert or sweets, is a "get together."

Example:

The Mediterranean Rendezvous—dramatic fabric
offsets appropriate serving pieces

Bellinis • A dry Italian Champagne • Tapenade
A wedge of Reggiano parmesan • A jar of roasted red peppers
Lots of great Italian bread • Toasted garbanzos • Artichoke Parmesan Spread
Yummy Mushroom Bruschetta • A pound of thinly sliced proscuitto

Assemble the entire food menu with matching plates and bowls
in the middle of the dining room table, and nosh and visit. This also
works on the coffee table or the kitchen counter.

CONTENTS

ANCHOVY-LESS TAPENADE

1 cup drained pitted black olives
1/4 cup drained rinsed capers
3 tablespoons extra-virgin olive oil
Juice of 1 lemon
Pepper to taste

Process the olives and capers in a food processor until finely chopped. Add the olive oil in a fine stream, processing until the mixture binds together. Add the lemon juice and pulse to combine. Season with pepper. Scoop into a serving bowl. Garnish with parsley leaves or sprigs. Guests spread this on carefully selected crackers or, even better, sliced French bread. SERVES 4

ARTICHOKE PARMESAN SPREAD

1 (12-ounce) can chopped artichoke hearts, drained
12 ounces Parmesan cheese, grated
1/2 cup half-and-half
1/4 teaspoon pepper

Combine the artichoke hearts, cheese, half-and-half and pepper in a bowl and mix well. Spoon into a buttered microwave-safe 1 1/2-quart oval baking dish. Microwave on High for 5 minutes. Bake at 350 degrees for 10 minutes or until brown and bubbly. Garnish with grape tomato halves, which are a delicious contrast. Serve warm and gooey with French bread, crackers or toast. SERVES 4 TO 6

BABA GHANNOUJH

1 (8- to 10-inch-long) eggplant
Juice of 2 lemons
4 parsley sprigs, stems removed
3 tablespoons tahini (sesame paste) or
 toasted sesame seeds
1 tablespoon oil-packed minced garlic
1/8 teaspoon salt, or to taste
1/8 teaspoon pepper

Cut the eggplant into halves lengthwise, leaving the skin on. Place on a baking sheet lined with foil. Bake at 400 degrees for 45 minutes. Scoop out the pulp, reserving the shells.

Process the eggplant pulp with the lemon juice, parsley, tahini, garlic, salt and pepper in a food processor until smooth. Spoon into the reserved eggplant shells. Chill, covered, in the refrigerator. Garnish with fresh cilantro. Serve with pita crisps.

MAKES VARIABLE SERVINGS

TIP: If you don't want to be careful or worry about the skin, discard it. Chill the mixture and serve in a lovely bowl that complements your theme or table setting! This can be prepared up to 24 hours in advance. Keep refrigerated until ready to serve.

CHILE CON QUESO

This is a great dip for a Super Bowl or patio party.

1 (1-pound) package Velveeta cheese
1 pound ground beef
1 (12-ounce) jar hot or mild salsa

Cut the cheese into 1-inch-thick slices. Brown the ground beef in a skillet, stirring until crumbly; drain. Stir in the salsa and bring to a simmer. Remove from the heat. Add a slice of cheese, stirring until the cheese is melted. Repeat with the remaining slices, reheating if it cools down too much to melt the cheese. Spoon into a serving bowl. This can be served with nacho chips, but I prefer it with less salty slices of French bread. We like this with Corona Mexican beer and lime as well as the Killer Frozen Margaritas (page 26) Susan Glahn is famous for! SERVES 12 TO 16

TIP: You cannot substitute another cheese for Velveeta or it will separate. Velveeta is really a very firm cheese sauce, not a cheese.

CUCUMBER DIP FOR SUMMER SHRIMP

1 cup fat-free sour cream
1 cup chilled coarsely chopped peeled cucumber
1/2 cup chopped parsley leaves
1/4 cup chopped dill leaves

Process the sour cream, cucumber, parsley and dill in a food processor until smooth. Spoon into a serving bowl. This makes 2 cups, which is enough for 1 1/2 pounds of shrimp. SERVES 4 TO 6 AS AN ENTRÉE OR 10 TO 12 AS PART OF ASSORTED APPETIZERS

FAUX MONTRACHET DIPPING SAUCE FOR ASPARAGUS

12 ounces Philadelphia or other fine cream cheese, softened
1 (8-ounce) bottle ranch salad dressing, such as Hidden Valley
1/2 teaspoon oil-packed minced garlic
1 handful of fresh parsley leaves (about 1/2 cup)
Salt and pepper to taste

Process the cream cheese, salad dressing and garlic in a food processor until smooth. Add the parsley and pulse until pretty and evenly distributed. Season with salt and pepper. SERVES 6 TO 10

SOUTHWESTERN SAMBA COOL VEGETABLE DIP

1 cup Hellmann's mayonnaise
1/2 cup chopped cilantro
1 teaspoon oil-packed minced garlic
2 tablespoons fresh lime juice
Pinch of white pepper

Process the mayonnaise, cilantro, garlic, lime juice and white pepper in a blender until smooth. Spoon into a serving bowl. SERVES 4 TO 6

VARIATION: You can also blend this into a 10- to 12-ounce can of drained black beans, add 1/2 tablespoon of chile powder, and you have a black bean dip!!! A turkey sandwich with Monterey Jack cheese and roasted red peppers out of a jar, dressed with samba sauce on good French bread, could be as satisfying as a STEAK! ANYBODY can do that!

TIP: Dips and dressings can also be used to make regular old sandwiches into distinctive signature food!

VEGGIE DIP BASE

Each part equals 8 ounces (1 cup) in the following recipes. Use Hellmann's, and only Hellmann's, mayonnaise. If you ever made mayonnaise from scratch, you would know it tastes exactly like Hellmann's, so let them do that step. It's OK to use plain yogurt or fat-free sour cream as a substitute for real sour cream, and it isn't even a sacrifice if you have the right mayo.

1 part sour cream
1 part Hellmann's mayonnaise

Combine the sour cream and mayonnaise in a bowl and mix well.

RUSSIAN VEGETABLE DIP

1 part Heinz catsup
1 tablespoon sweet relish
Squeeze of fresh lemon juice

Combine the Veggie Dip Base, catsup, relish and lemon juice in a bowl and mix well.

DIJON VEGETABLE DIP

1 tablespoon Dijon mustard
1/4 teaspoon salt
1/2 teaspoon sugar

Combine the Veggie Dip Base, Dijon mustard, salt and sugar in a bowl and mix well.

LOUISIANA LOUIS VEGETABLE DIP

1 part chili sauce
1 teaspoon paprika
1/2 teaspoon pepper
1/2 small onion, minced

Combine the Veggie Dip Base, chili sauce, paprika, pepper and onion in a bowl and mix well. Chill, covered, for 8 to 12 hours to enhance the flavor.

HORSERADISH DIP, SAUCE OR DRESSING

2 tablespoons prepared horseradish
1/2 teaspoon salt
1/2 teaspoon white pepper

Combine the Veggie Dip Base, horseradish, salt and white pepper in a bowl and mix well.

PÂTÉ DUXELLE

Pâté duxelle is an excellent recipe to serve to all kinds of people and large groups as well. The finished product ends up being like Yummy Mushroom Bruschetta (page 23) without the "on bread" assembly. In this case, each person spreads his or her own!!!

1/2 cup (1 stick) salted butter
1 pound mushrooms, rinsed and patted dry
1 onion, coarsely chopped
2 chicken bouillon cubes
1/2 teaspoon pepper
2 tablespoons dry bread crumbs

Heat the butter in a skillet until melted. Add the mushrooms, onion and chicken bouillon cubes. Sauté until the onion is tender. Remove from the heat and let stand until cool. Process in a food processor with the pepper and bread crumbs. Spoon into a serving bowl. Serve warm with crackers, bread or breadsticks. SERVES 6 TO 8

NOTE: If you use three times as many bread crumbs, this can be used to stuff chicken, pork chops, or mushroom caps. On another occasion, layer the duxelle between thin slices of fresh zucchini and cover with store-bought spaghetti sauce. Bake as a vegetarian entrée or side dish. Another time, you might enjoy the duxelle layered with fresh spinach and sliced tomatoes as a bed for white-fleshed fish...pour a cup of white wine over this before you put it in the oven. The options are endless.

SPICY COCKTAIL GARBANZOS

1 (16-ounce) can garbanzo beans, drained
1 tablespoon extra-virgin olive oil
1 tablespoon oil-packed minced garlic
1/2 teaspoon salt
1/2 teaspoon cumin
1/2 teaspoon pepper
1/2 teaspoon paprika

Line a baking sheet with parchment paper. Toss the beans with olive oil and garlic in a bowl. Add the salt and toss to combine. Add the cumin and toss to combine. Add the pepper and toss to combine. Add the paprika and toss to combine.

Spread the bean mixture evenly over the prepared baking sheet. Bake at 400 degrees for 25 to 30 minutes or until dry and light brown. These are really good warm with drinks but are even better at room temperature. MAKES 2 CUPS

SAUTÉED BLACK PEPPER BRIE

Once again, this is as easy (almost) as taking a pizza out of a box!

1 (8-ounce) round of Brie
2 teaspoons coarsely ground pepper
1 teaspoon butter

Sprinkle water over the Brie. Sprinkle the pepper over the top of the Brie. Heat the butter in a skillet over medium heat until melted. Add the Brie and cook until bubbly; do not burn. Turn to cook the other side or place brown side up on a plate. Serve with apple slices, crackers or grape tomatoes (my favorite) and French bread.

If you have trouble getting the pepper to stay on, simply sprinkle it in the pan, then add the Brie. SERVES 4 TO 6

NOTE: Alternative flavorings for Brie are unending. Use rosemary instead of pepper or dried thyme, or for a seasonal change…pair with whole cranberries or purchased chutney…or let blue cheese crumbles melt over it when just out of the skillet.

GOOEY CRAB PIZZA

Early in my career, I received a mailing from a newly opened restaurant announcing that they were the home of the "soon-to-be-famous Crab Meat Gooeys." I nearly dropped dead—this was our internal reference to our beloved "Hot Crab Canapés." I had been making the dish for eight years since I developed the idea out of leftovers when I was in my early twenties. One of my staff was so enraged that she called the owner to ask how they could base their reputation on "my item" without my permission. They informed her that it had nothing to do with me; they had gotten the idea from Virginia Rainey...who they did not know was my general manager! Nevertheless, the concept works in a variety of ways. Crab pizza is one of them that is currently in vogue, and the possibilities of the procedure are endless.

1 (8-ounce) can lump crab meat, drained
12 ounces Philadelphia or other fine cream cheese, softened
3 scallions, white part only, thinly sliced
4 (1-ounce) slices imported Swiss cheese, chopped
1/2 teaspoon coarsely ground pepper
1 tablespoon grated Parmesan cheese
2 tablespoons Hellmann's mayonnaise
5 English muffins, split

Preheat the oven to 400 degrees. Combine the crab meat, cream cheese, scallions, Swiss cheese, pepper, Parmesan cheese and mayonnaise in a bowl and mix well. Spread liberally over each muffin half almost to the edge. Place on a baking sheet. Bake for 10 minutes or until puffy and starting to brown. Let stand for 5 minutes. Cut each muffin half into quarters. SERVES 4 TO 5

MANHATTAN LEFTOVER SALMON BRUSCHETTA

1 (4-inch-diameter) loaf Italian or Cuban bread
8 ounces Philadelphia cream cheese, softened
1 (6- to 8-ounce) salmon fillet, cooked and cooled, left over from dinner
2 tablespoons Hellmann's mayonnaise
2 tablespoons lemon juice
2 tablespoons grated Parmesan cheese
Pinch of white pepper
1/2 teaspoon tiny capers
2 tablespoons chopped fresh dill
Chopped chives (optional)

Cut the bread into 3/4-inch-thick slices. Place on a baking sheet. Bake at 300 degrees for 12 minutes or until toasted, turning once. You may also toast in a toaster with wide slots. You may prepare the toast up to 4 hours ahead.

Combine the cream cheese, salmon, mayonnaise, lemon juice, Parmesan cheese, white pepper, capers and dill in a bowl and mix well; the mixture will be lumpy. Spread 1/4 inch thick over 1 side of each of the toasts. Place on a baking sheet.

Broil on low with the oven door open until bubbly and beginning to brown. Sprinkle with chives. Let stand until cooled slightly. Cut into equal pieces and serve.

SERVES 8 TO 12

YUMMY MUSHROOM BRUSCHETTA

This appetizer is just a slightly fancier version of garlic bread. You can add a little pesto instead of thyme...chopped pine nuts if you prefer...remember—it's just a procedure!

1 large loaf French bread
1/4 cup (1/2 stick) butter
2 cups sliced mushrooms
1 cup (4 ounces) grated Parmesan cheese
1 teaspoon oil-packed minced garlic
1/2 teaspoon thyme
1/2 teaspoon pepper

Cut the bread lengthwise into halves and place on a baking sheet. Bake at 375 degrees for 10 minutes. Heat the butter in a skillet until melted. Add the mushrooms. Sauté until tender (they will be quite wet). Combine the cooked mushrooms, cheese, garlic, thyme and pepper in a bowl and mix well.

Spread the mushroom mixture over the cut sides of the bread. Bake for 10 minutes. Cut into slices and place on a serving plate. Serve with drinks. This is very filling, vegetarian, rich and satisfying—it serves a lot of purposes. SERVES 8 TO 10

EASY CHEDDAR CRISPS

1/2 cup (1 stick) salted butter, softened
1 pound Cheddar cheese, shredded
1 cup flour
1/4 teaspoon cayenne pepper
1 cup crisp rice cereal

Combine the butter, cheese, flour, cayenne pepper and cereal in a bowl and mix well. Drop by teaspoonfuls onto a nonstick baking sheet. Bake at 350 degrees for 20 minutes or until they begin to brown....KEEP YOUR EYES ON THEM. These last a week when stored in glass or metal—less in plastic.

COSMOPOLITAN CHEDDAR CRISPS

1/2 cup (2 ounces) grated Parmesan cheese
1 pound extra-sharp Cheddar cheese, shredded
1/2 cup (1 stick) salted butter, softened
1/2 teaspoon cayenne pepper
2 cups flour
Kosher salt

Combine the Parmesan cheese, Cheddar cheese, butter and cayenne pepper in a mixing bowl and mix well, adding 1/2 teaspoonfuls of water if needed to moisten (some cheese is wetter than others). Add the flour, mixing until the mixture forms a ball. Roll or press out by hand on a lightly floured surface. Cut into strips and place on a baking sheet. Bake at 350 degrees for 15 to 20 minutes or until the edges begin to brown. Press in kosher salt crystals while hot. These last a week when stored in glass or metal—less in plastic. MAKES 2 DOZEN CRISPS

THE STONE FENCE

Destined to be a fall favorite.

1/2 gallon freshly pressed cider
2 cups Stolichnaya cinnamon vodka
2 cups applejack

Stir the cider, vodka and applejack together in a punch bowl and mix well. Ladle into glasses. You may combine 1 cup cider, 1 to 2 tablespoons vodka and 1 tablespoon applejack in a 12-ounce glass to make 1 drink. MAKES 40 (1/2-CUP) DRINKS

NOTE: According to my Mom, in the 1940s, this was called "Kickapoo juice" and was inspired by the comic strip Li'l Abner.

LONG ISLAND "TEA"

1 cup tequila
1 cup rum
1 cup vodka
1 cup gin
1 cup Triple Sec
2 cups sour mix or lemonade
2 cups cola
Ice

Stir the tequila, rum, vodka, gin, Triple Sec, sour mix and cola together in a pitcher. Refrigerate, covered, until chilled through. Pour into glasses filled with ice. This is very alcoholic! You may pour into a 1-gallon container filled with ice.
MAKES 18 (1/2-CUP) DRINKS

KAHLÚA PUNCH BOWL

This is a centerpiece beverage—wonderful for a shower. It is really a cocktail punch bowl, and one who likes Kahlúa and cream will LOVE this. It saves a lot of work when you are having a group. You can skip the ice cream and serve it for a late brunch.

8 cups half-and-half
4 cups Kahlúa
4 cups medium strength brewed coffee, chilled
Pinch of cinnamon, or to taste
1 cup crème de cacao
1 (1/2-gallon) carton coffee ice cream
Ice

Combine the half-and-half, Kahlúa, coffee, cinnamon and crème de cacao in a punch bowl and mix well. Scoop the ice cream into the punch bowl. Serve over ice.
MAKES 1 GALLON

KILLER FROZEN MARGARITAS

One fifth of Jose Cuervo Especial tequila
2 cups Triple Sec
4 (6-ounce) cans limeade
7 cups water

Set aside 1 cup of the tequila and reserve for another use. Combine the remaining tequila, Triple Sec, limeade and water in a 1 1/2-gallon plastic container and mix well. Freeze, covered, for 3 days or longer. Remove from the freezer and let stand for 1 hour. Stir; the mixture will be slushy. MAKES 1 1/2 GALLONS

SOUR APPLE MARTINI

This is straight alcohol at room temperature. Poured over ice, within minutes, the drink is 50 percent alcohol and 50 percent water. However, it is still a "sippin'" cocktail...not a quaffing drink. It is extremely refreshing, not sweet, and appropriate for summer, winter, spring, and fall. It is incredibly easy, unusual, and a true martini!

Ice
2 ounces DeKuyper Sour Apple Pucker
2 ounces Stolichnaya or other excellent vodka

Pack a 6-ounce martini glass with ice. Add the liqueur and vodka and stir to combine. MAKES 1 DRINK

THE TRUE OCEAN VIEW MARTINI

This is a great punch bowl recipe, and you can still use martini glasses for effect. It's very strong, so use lots of ice. I like to pour a little extra curaçao in the bottom of the martini glass, giving the illusion of deepening water.

Juice of 1 lemon
2 cups Skyy Citrus vodka
1/2 cup blue curaçao
Ice

Combine the lemon juice, vodka, liqueur and ice in a 1-quart pitcher and stir to combine. Garnish with thin lemon slices and serve in large martini glasses that have been packed with ice. As they dilute, they cool you and get less strong.

TIP: If you like your martinis strong, keep the alcohol in the freezer but still pour the liqueur over the ice. If you want weaker martinis, keep the alcohol at room temperature to encourage dilution.

PEACH SOURS

Country Time lemonade
2 cups peach schnapps
2 tablespoons grenadine
Ice

Prepare 1 quart of lemonade in a 2-quart pitcher according to the package directions, using slightly less water. Stir in the schnapps and grenadine. Pour into glasses over ice. Garnish with peach or orange slices. Increase fourfold for punch bowls. You may substitute Crystal Light lemonade for the Country Time lemonade to reduce the sugar content. You may substitute amaretto for the schnapps and orange juice for the grenadine for Amaretto Sours. Or substitute apricot brandy for the schnapps and orange juice for the grenadine for Apricot Sours. MAKES 16 (1/2-CUP) DRINKS

THE BEST BELLINI

The Bellini was invented in Harry's Bar in Venice from fresh peach purée and Champagne. It is wonderful! This is a pretty admirable imitation.

1 (12-ounce) package frozen peach slices
1/4 cup confectioners' sugar
4 cups white wine

Process the peaches, confectioners' sugar and wine in a blender until smooth and slushy. Pour into martini glasses. MAKES ABOUT 8 (1/2-CUP) DRINKS

PIÑA COLADAS

Ice
1 (12-ounce) can Coco López cream of coconut
1¹/2 cups prepared Country Time lemonade
1¹/2 cups pineapple juice
³/4 cup spiced or dark rum

Spoon the ice into glasses. Stir the cream of coconut, lemonade, pineapple juice and rum together in a pitcher. Pour over the ice and serve. For Frozen Piña Coladas, fill a blender half full with ice, increase the cream of coconut to 2 cups, add a little extra lemonade concentrate, increase the rum to 1 cup and process until smooth and slushy. MAKES 4 OR 5 (12-OUNCE) DRINKS

TROPICAL CARIBBEAN COLADA COOLER

2 (12-ounce) cans mango nectar
2 (12-ounce) cans guava nectar
2 (12-ounce) cans passion fruit nectar
2 (12-ounce) cans pineapple nectar
1 (12-ounce) can Coco López cream of coconut
1 cup freshly squeezed Key lime or lemon juice
4 cups Bacardi Gold rum

Combine the mango nectar, guava nectar, passion fruit nectar, pineapple nectar, cream of coconut, Key lime juice and rum in a punch bowl and mix well. Combine equal amounts of punch and ice in a glass and serve or process in a blender until slushy. Add 4 cups water to the punch if it is to be chilled and served over ice in a glass to balance the dilution taking place in a punch bowl. This can be made the day before and chilled. It is exotic without being too odd! Garnish with paper parasols if you want your guests transported; a fresh pineapple wedge can work, too! MAKES ABOUT 40 (1/2-CUP) DRINKS

RED WINE COOLER

This is very good, very easy, and not very alcoholic.

Dry red wine
Sprite
Lemon juice

Stir equal parts of wine and Sprite together in a glass. Stir in a small amount of lemon juice. Garnish with lemon, lime or orange slices. MAKES VARIABLE SERVINGS

T IP: In a glass pitcher, garnish with lemon, lime and orange slices...very colorful and flavorful! To turn it into sangria, cut the Sprite in half and add 1/4 teaspoon nutmeg and 1/4 teaspoon cinnamon.

SIZZLE SWIZZLE

A backyard rum punch so you don't have to have a full bar, just beer, wine, and a very special specialty drink.

1 cup lemonade
1 cup each orange juice and pineapple juice
1/2 cup Captain Morgan's Spiced rum
1/2 cup amaretto

Stir the lemonade, orange juice, pineapple juice, rum and amaretto together in a punch bowl. Ladle into glasses. Garnish with cherries and orange slices. For a group, change the cups to quarts! MAKES 8 (1/2-CUP) DRINKS

AMARETTO PLANTATION PUNCH

This is a very old-fashioned recipe that your grandmother will love!

1 (3-ounce) package tangerine gelatin
2 cups hot water
2 tablespoons almond extract
8 cups orange juice
8 cups pineapple juice

Dissolve the gelatin in the hot water in a punch bowl. Stir in the almond extract. Pour in the orange juice and pineapple juice and mix well. Serve over ice. You may substitute tea for the pineapple juice and sweeten to taste with sugar.
MAKES 2 GALLONS

CHEERY CHERRY BIRTHDAY PARTY GIGGLE

2 packages cherry gelatin
4 cups boiling water
1 mini tub Crystal Light lemonade mix
8 cups cold water
1 cup (or more) maraschino cherry juice
1/2 cup grenadine
Ice

Dissolve the gelatin in the boiling water in a punch bowl. Stir in the lemonade mix. Add the cold water, cherry juice and grenadine and mix well. Add lots of ice and let stand for 15 minutes. Garnish with lemon slices and maraschino cherries.
MAKES 2 GALLONS

SIMPLY SWEETS AND BORDERLINE BAKING

Once you have digested my nontraditional viewpoint in Chapter One, you will probably believe I am not interested in serving dessert. Not true— this is the biggest chapter in the book! The key is don't try to do everything, all the time. Extreme effort is what makes the process tiresome. It is what makes us avoid giving any of our time to entertaining, because we feel we end up giving ALL of it.

This being said, the sweetest way to communicate your love is by example. Just as visiting at home before you go out to dinner is an option, you can just as easily get together at home afterward for dessert and coffee or Champagne. Late Sunday afternoon open house with Kahlúa Punch, coffee, and Champagne is different...imaginative, and items you have prepared can readily be combined with those you have skillfully purchased. Selections in this chapter can also make a basic breakfast into a lovely brunch. Or, think how your kids will feel when you pull out a macadamia-crusted coconut cream pie you made on computer break at home, even if it is served after the carry-out Chinese your spouse picked up!

*Example: Spiced Merlot Sorbet after ordered-in pizza and your fabulous salad. Friday night after work, four of you meet for Mexican, then adjourn to your house for a few rounds of cards followed by your (wow!) Praline Banana Cheesecake (or even the modified Au Yea ice cream). Your weekend will seem so much longer because you used Friday; it was memorable because of **your** dessert!!! (And your friends felt honored and nurtured by your effort.)*

These plans result in minimal cleanup, and for young families, adults on fixed incomes, and starting-out singles, a very limited financial commitment! When you think of ways to interact without overwhelming yourself or overcommitting...you get it! This goes for grandparents, neighbors, friends, and lovers. A homemade dessert or a baked item is always regarded as a treasure.

CONTENTS

CANDIED FRUIT

I like this because I rarely see it done. Use a seasonal fruit. You can serve it with store-bought cake, sorbet, cookies, or ice cream, and let a few minutes of your time steal the show! This isn't really easy, but it's fun.

1/2 **cup water**
1 **cup sugar**
1 **cup fresh fruit, such as sliced apples, grapes, blueberries,**
    cranberries, sliced peaches, banana pieces or pineapple pieces

Line a baking sheet with parchment paper. Combine the water and sugar in a saucepan and mix well. Bring to a boil, stirring constantly. Cook for 4 to 5 minutes or to 238 degrees on a candy thermometer, soft-ball stage, stirring constantly. Remove from the heat. Stir in the fruit. Let stand for 30 seconds. Remove the fruit and place on the prepared baking sheet, taking care to have each piece separate from the others as they cool. Let stand until cool. Do not use strawberries, melons, canned fruit, plums or oranges because their water content is too high and they have insufficient surface density. MAKES 1 CUP

NOTE: This has to be done on the day you want to serve it, so I would recommend that you first try it on a day when it doesn't matter.

CANDIED PECANS

1/2 **cup packed brown sugar**
1/2 **cup granulated sugar**
1/2 **cup water**
1 **teaspoon vanilla extract**
2 **cups pecan halves**

Combine the brown sugar, granulated sugar, water and vanilla in a heavy saucepan and mix well. Cook for 10 to 15 minutes, stirring gently. Add the pecan halves; do not break the pecans. Cook until the liquid is almost gone; do not burn. Pour in an even layer onto a nonstick baking sheet. Separate the pecan halves. Let stand until cool. MAKES 2 CUPS

TIP: You can candy walnuts, filberts, cashews, and peanuts. You can add spices like cinnamon or nutmeg in small quantities if you wish.

ADULT COFFEE ICE CREAM AU YEA

1 pint coffee ice cream, slightly softened
2 Heath candy bars, broken into pieces
1/4 cup rum
2 teaspoons brewed instant coffee

Combine the ice cream, candy bars, rum and coffee in a food processor. Pulse 10 to 12 times for 2 seconds each time. Spoon into a container and freeze.
MAKES 4 SERVINGS

VARIATIONS: To vanilla ice cream, add Cognac, cinnamon, apples, and caramel sauce;
(OR) crème de menthe, white chocolate chips, and dark chocolate chips;
(OR) vodka, cranberry relish, and walnuts;
(OR) rum (or port), almonds, orange peel, and raisins;
(OR) pineapple, pecans, coconut, and chopped bananas.

To chocolate ice cream, add Kahlúa, a chocolate bar, pecans, and coconut;
(OR) crème de cacao, 2 tablespoons peanut butter or peanuts, and 1 banana;
(OR) Kahlúa, 1/2 cup white chocolate chips, and 2 tablespoons macadamia nuts.

SPICED MERLOT SORBET

Use cinnamon in fall, fresh orange zest in summer...a lovely palate cleanser easily accomplished.

1 cup sugar
1 cup water
2 cups red wine, such as merlot
2 cinnamon sticks
1 (2-inch) piece of orange peel

Combine the sugar and water in a saucepan and mix well. Cook until the sugar is dissolved. Add the wine. Bring to a simmer. Add the cinnamon sticks and orange peel. Bring to a low boil and boil for 5 minutes. Let stand to enhance the flavor. Strain and let stand until cool. Pour into an ice cream freezer container. Freeze using the manufacturer's directions. MAKES 4 CUPS

NOTE: Adjust the quantities to your machine's capacity.

TIP: I once used a tin of pear nectar and once mango in lieu of spice or orange. I always like it! If you use juice, reduce the water by 1/2 cup for every 1/2 cup nectar used. This is very easy but never expected. I think an automatic ice cream freezer is a *very* worthwhile investment.

BEAUTIFUL BUTTERSCOTCH CARAMEL

1 1/4 cups packed light brown sugar
3/4 cup light corn syrup
1/4 cup (1/2 stick) salted butter
3 tablespoons water
1 1/2 teaspoons vanilla extract
1/2 cup heavy cream

Combine the brown sugar, corn syrup, butter and water in a 3-quart heavy saucepan. Bring to a boil, stirring constantly. Reduce the heat and boil for 5 minutes; do not stir and do not taste. Remove from the heat. Stir in the vanilla. Let stand for 5 minutes. Stir gently. Stir in the cream about 1 tablespoon at a time. The sauce will become smooth, glossy and a bit thicker—more "caramel-like." When served over ice cream, this is so delicious and just the right weight—it won't run to the bottom or clump up. MAKES 2 TO 2 1/2 CUPS

NOTE: This is also great on sliced peaches, rice pudding, or sautéed apples with cinnamon, as a dip for cookies, or with fruit slices like a caramel fondue! You can also melt two Hershey bars (the flat milk chocolate ones) into it in the microwave and stir up a chocolate caramel sauce...and it's also very flavorful for dipping strawberries (after cooling it slightly).

SPECIAL PEAR HALVES WITH HONEYED CREAM

1 cup red wine, preferably dry
Juice of 1 orange
1/4 cup red currant jelly
4 cloves
1 cinnamon stick
1 large can Bartlett pear halves, drained

Combine the wine, orange juice, jelly, cloves and cinnamon in a microwave-safe bowl. Microwave on High for 2 minutes. Add the pears. Let stand, covered, for 2 hours until cool. Chill for 4 hours or longer; drain. Arrange on a platter and garnish with whole cloves, cinnamon sticks and orange slices. Serve with Honeyed Cream (page 41).

You may add peach halves, apricot halves or maraschino cherries if desired. You may also add 1/2 cup Grand Marnier, Frangelico or amaretto. You may substitute 1/4 cup Cognac for the wine. SERVES 4

HONEYED CREAM

1 cup Cool Whip
1/2 cup vanilla yogurt
3 tablespoons sugar-free pancake syrup

Combine the Cool Whip, yogurt and syrup in a bowl and mix gently.
MAKES ABOUT 1 1/2 CUPS

NOTE: This is a great fruit dip if you add 3 tablespoons Cognac or rum. There will be an interesting chemical reaction. The sauce will tighten up into a sauce the weight of "Romanoff"—it's very rich.

LOVELY LEMON CHANTILLY

This is a real recipe if you're ready for it...but only one step, more than assembly, but very manageable.

2 cups whipping cream, chilled
1/2 cup superfine sugar
1/4 cup freshly squeezed lemon juice, chilled (about 3 or 4 lemons)
1 teaspoon lemon zest (yellow part only), chilled

Beat the cream, sugar, lemon juice and lemon zest in a chilled mixing bowl until very thick. Pour into a serving bowl or individual serving dishes. Chill until ready to serve. Garnish with thin lemon slices and fresh mint leaves. SERVES 4

MOCHA MAYHEM...A SINFUL DESSERT FINISH

This takes less than five minutes to produce, and it's really cooking!

1/2 **cup brewed coffee**
2 **ounces semisweet chocolate, broken into pieces**
1/2 **teaspoon vanilla extract**
1/4 **teaspoon cornstarch**
Sugar to taste

Combine half of the coffee, the chocolate and vanilla in a saucepan and mix well. Cook over low heat until the mixture is melted and hot. Combine the remaining coffee with the cornstarch in a cup and add to the chocolate mixture. Cook until steaming, stirring constantly; do not boil. Stir in the sugar to taste. Let stand until slightly cool. You may add cinnamon in the winter, sliced almonds and/or raisins in the fall, chopped maraschino cherries anytime, or a few drops of Cognac in front of the fire. SERVES 2

ONE-MINUTE CHOCOLATE MOUSSE

This recipe was the beginning of my appreciation of "instant results" cooking. I knew how to make mousse from scratch and had done it successfully—surprisingly, this was just as good and required about ten percent of the effort. As with many renditions of popular dishes, I have no idea where the original shortcut mousse came from. This one is modified slightly from my first try, and I hope you like it!

2 eggs
1 1/2 cups half-and-half
2 cups semisweet chocolate chips, at room temperature
Pinch of cinnamon
1 to 3 teaspoons Grand Marnier, rum, Frangelico, amaretto or Cognac

Place the uncracked eggs in a bowl. Add enough hot water to cover and set aside. Heat the half-and-half in a saucepan until steaming; do not boil.

Crack the eggs into a blender. Add the chocolate chips and cinnamon. Pulse 10 times or process for 30 seconds. Add the steaming half-and-half and process for 45 seconds. Add the Grand Marnier and process for 15 seconds. Chill, covered, in the refrigerator. Serve with shortbread cookies or French vanilla cigarette russe.
SERVES 6

NOTE: To make this mousse a chocolate walnut pie, sprinkle 2 cups of chopped walnuts evenly over the bottom of a graham cracker crust. Pour the mousse over the walnuts. Bake at 350 degrees for 20 minutes; the center will be puffy. Chill in the refrigerator. You may substitute pecans, peanuts, cashews, or hazelnuts for the walnuts.

MACADAMIA COCONUT CRUST

1/2 cup crushed macadamia nuts (crush like crumbs)
8 whole graham crackers, crushed
1/2 cup sweetened flaked coconut
1/2 cup (1 stick) butter, melted

Combine the macadamia nut crumbs, graham cracker crumbs, coconut and butter in a bowl and mix well. Press over the bottom of a pie shell. Fill with One-Minute Chocolate Mousse, vanilla pudding prepared from a mix, or for a tropical dessert…Key lime pie filling drizzled with a purée of fresh mango, or even the cheesecake recipes within this chapter. MAKES 1 PIECRUST

COMPANY'S COMING PEACH PIE

1 unbaked (9-inch) pie shell
1 tablespoon butter, melted
2 teaspoons vanilla extract
8 ounces Philadelphia cream cheese, at room temperature
1/4 cup sugar
1/4 cup sour cream
1/2 cup apricot preserves
1 (16-ounce) can sliced red freestone peaches

Brush the pie shell with the butter. Bake according to the package directions. Let stand until cool. Process the vanilla, cream cheese, sugar, sour cream and 1/4 cup of the preserves in a blender until smooth. Pour into the baked pie shell.

Arrange the peaches artfully in a spoke pattern over the top. Drizzle the remaining 1/4 cup preserves over the peaches. Chill in the refrigerator. SERVES 6

NUTMEG CUSTARD APPLE PIE

If you like crème brûlée, you will probably love this dessert!

2 cups dehydrated apples
3 cups water
1 tablespoon sugar
1 tablespoon white or brown raisins
1/2 cup chopped pecans or walnuts
1 (9-inch) frozen pie shell, thawed
3 eggs
2 cups milk
2 teaspoons vanilla extract
1/2 cup sugar
1 teaspoon cinnamon
Pinch of salt
1/4 teaspoon nutmeg

Cook the apples and water in a medium saucepan over medium heat for 15 minutes. Remove from the heat. Stir in 1 tablespoon sugar and the raisins. Press the pecans evenly into the bottom of the pie shell. Spread the apple mixture over the pecans.

Beat the eggs, milk, vanilla, 1/2 cup sugar, cinnamon, salt and nutmeg in a mixing bowl. Pour over the apple mixture. Bake at 350 degrees until the center has risen and is brown. SERVES 6

NOTE: You may combine the apples and water in a bowl and chill overnight. Heat in a saucepan for 5 minutes. To use fresh apples: Cut 2 peeled apples into 1/4-inch slices and toss in lemon juice until coated. Microwave for 2 to 3 minutes or until softened.

PACKY JOHNSON'S RASPBERRY RAZZLE-DAZZLE COOKIES

3/4 cups (1 1/2 sticks) margarine, softened
1/4 cup sugar
1/4 teaspoon salt
1/4 teaspoon almond extract
1 egg
1 1/2 cups flour
1 cup red raspberry preserves
1/2 cup flaked coconut
1/2 cup nuts
Marshmallow Fluff

Preheat the oven to 350 degrees. Beat the margarine, sugar and salt in a mixing bowl until light and fluffy. Add the almond extract, egg and flour and beat until a dough forms. Pat over the bottom of a 9×13-inch baking pan. Bake for 15 minutes.

Reduce the oven temperature to 300 degrees.Spread the preserves over the hot baked layer. Sprinkle the coconut over the preserves. Sprinkle the nuts over the coconut. Drop the marshmallow fluff by teaspoonfuls evenly over the nuts. Bake for 15 minutes. Cut into bars. MAKES 2 DOZEN BARS

NO-BAKE SWEETHEART COOKIES

1 (6-ounce) package semisweet chocolate chips
1/2 cup sugar
2 tablespoons light corn syrup
1/2 cup Frangelico, crème de noyaux or amaretto
10 ounces vanilla wafers, coarsely crushed
1 cup finely chopped almonds
Confectioners' sugar

Heat the chocolate chips in a microwave-safe bowl in the microwave until melted. Stir in the sugar. Add the corn syrup and Frangelico and mix well. Combine the wafer crumbs and almonds in a bowl and mix well. Drizzle in the chocolate mixture and mix to bind.

Shape the mixture into dime-size balls. Roll in confectioners' sugar to coat. Serve immediately or freeze in a metal tin to avoid moisture from condensation.

MAKES ABOUT 2 DOZEN COOKIES

TUSCAN SHORTCAKE

This is an adaptation of an old complicated recipe of Italian origin. I have simplified it to enjoy on the balcony of my dear friend Leon's beautiful Tuscan villa. Easy enough for preparation on vacation. For an authentic Italian experience, eat this and sip Prosecco during sunset...prego.

3 cups self-rising flour
1 1/4 cups sugar
1/4 teaspoon salt
2 egg yolks
1 1/2 cups half-and-half
1 teaspoon vanilla extract
1 teaspoon almond extract
1/2 teaspoon anise seeds (optional)
1/2 teaspoon grated orange zest (optional)

Preheat the oven to 350 degrees. Process the flour, sugar and salt in a food processor for 5 to 10 seconds. Add the egg yolks, half-and-half, vanilla, almond extract, anise seeds and orange zest to the flour mixture and process for 30 seconds.

Pour the batter over the bottom of a 6×9-inch baking pan sprayed with nonstick cooking spray. Bake until the top begins to brown. Let stand until cool. Cut into slices.

TOO-BUSY BANANA BREAD

1 cup (2 sticks) butter, softened
1 cup sugar
4 ripe bananas
2 eggs
2 cups milk
1 cup chopped pecans or pecan meal (optional)
2 cups self-rising flour

Beat the butter and sugar in a mixing bowl until light and fluffy. Add the bananas and beat until fluffy. Add the eggs and beat until fluffy. Add the milk and mix well. Stir in the pecans. Beat in the flour at low speed.

Pour the batter into a greased nonstick loaf pan. Bake at 350 degrees for 1 hour.
MAKES 1 LOAF

CINNAMON (MONKEY) BREAD

3/4 cup sugar
2 tablespoons cinnamon
4 (8-count) cans Pillsbury Grands or other good quality biscuits
1/2 cup (1 stick) butter
1 tablespoon cream
1 cup packed brown sugar

Combine the sugar and cinnamon in a brown paper lunch sack and shake to combine, holding the sack closed. Cut each biscuit into quarters. Place 8 biscuit pieces in the sack and shake to coat, holding the sack closed. Place the coated biscuit pieces in a buttered bundt pan. Repeat the process until all the biscuit pieces have been used.

Place the butter, cream and brown sugar in a microwave-safe bowl. Heat in the microwave until bubbly. Pour over the biscuit pieces. Bake at 325 degrees for 45 to 55 minutes. SERVES 12 TO 16

NOTE: These breads are called "monkey" presumably because they can be pulled apart by hand. I did not invent this, but I don't know who did. My mom did a garlic bread rendition of this when we were entertaining a gang!! As you may have guessed, you, too, could alter the shake process by using herbs or garlic powder for your own rendition!!

BASIC COFFEE CAKE OR MUFFIN BATTER

2 cups self-rising flour
1/2 cup sugar
3/4 teaspoon salt
2 eggs
3/4 cup milk or buttermilk
1/2 cup (1 stick) butter, softened
3/4 to 11/2 cups blueberries, chocolate chips, raisins
 with a pinch of cinnamon, or the additive of your choice

Combine the flour, sugar, salt, eggs, milk and butter in a bowl and mix well. Stir in the desired amount of the addition you chose.

For muffins, fill greased muffin cups 2/3 full. Bake at 375 degrees for 20 minutes. For miniature muffins, reduce the baking time.

For coffee cake, pour the batter into a greased baking pan. Bake at 325 degrees for 40 minutes or until a wooden pick inserted in the center comes out clean. SERVES 12

CARAMEL APPLE BREAD PUDDING

If you live in a cool climate, this is a fantastic fall indulgence. Even in the south, where we like to simulate seasonal variation, this could be an alternate to plum pudding at Christmas.

2 tablespoons brown sugar
8 slices good quality white bread, such as Pepperidge Farm
2 tart apples, peeled and chopped
1/2 cup brown or golden raisins
2 tablespoons brown sugar
2 tablespoons butter, cut into small pieces
2 cups half-and-half
1 cup sugar
4 eggs
2 teaspoons cinnamon
1 teaspoon nutmeg
1/8 teaspoon salt
4 to 8 pieces butter
1/4 cup packed brown sugar

Butter a 7×11-inch baking dish liberally, leaving little bits of butter here and there. Sprinkle 2 tablespoons brown sugar over the butter. Remove the crusts from the bread. Tear into pieces and arrange evenly in the prepared dish. Sprinkle the apples and raisins evenly over the bread pieces. Sprinkle 2 tablespoons brown sugar unevenly over the apples and raisins. Sprinkle the butter pieces over the brown sugar.

Combine the half-and-half, sugar, eggs, cinnamon, nutmeg and salt in a bowl, blender or food processor and mix well. Pour over the layers, tilting the dish to soak the bread and leaving the apples and raisins evenly distributed.

Place 4 to 8 pieces butter around the top. Sprinkle 1/4 cup brown sugar evenly over the layers. Bake at 350 degrees for 45 minutes or until firm and fluffy in the middle.
SERVES 10 TO 12

BAKED RICE PUDDING

Easy...can be done ahead of time. Once, I made this delicious, warm, rich rice pudding in the same week we got a puppy...my children asked if I was going to have another baby!! I guess they liked this, but it only tastes *like a special occasion.*

1 cup arborio rice
4 cups milk
1/2 cup sugar
1/4 teaspoon salt
1/4 teaspoon nutmeg
1 teaspoon cinnamon
1/2 teaspoon vanilla extract

Preheat the oven to 325 degrees. Combine the rice, milk, sugar, salt, nutmeg, cinnamon and vanilla in a bowl and stir just until the spices are mixed in and the sugar has almost dissolved. Pour the pudding into a buttered 1 1/2-quart baking dish at least 3 inches deep. Bake for 1 1/2 hours, stirring after the first 30 minutes and every 20 minutes after that. SERVES 4 TO 6

VARIATIONS: Stir in 1/2 cup raisins and an additional 1/2 cup milk to the rice mixture before baking. The additional milk keeps the pudding creamy because the raisins absorb a lot of moisture.

Stir 3 mashed overripe bananas into the rice mixture before baking. Serve the pudding warm with lots of white chocolate shavings.

Double the spices and stir drained sliced peaches into the rice mixture before baking. Combine 1 cup chopped pecans, 1 cup packed brown sugar and 2 tablespoons melted butter in a bowl and mix well. Sprinkle over the top of the baked pudding. Broil under a preheated broiler for 1 minute or until the topping begins to bubble. Turn off the broiler and move the pudding to a lower oven rack. Let stand for 5 minutes. Now it's a totally different dessert!

FASTER SWEDISH BAKED RICE PUDDING

1¹/2 cups Uncle Ben's converted rice
2¹/4 cups water
¹/2 teaspoon salt
¹/2 cup sugar
¹/2 teaspoon ground cardamom
    (optional, but it makes it Swedish)
4 cups milk
2 eggs, beaten
1 teaspoon almond extract
1 teaspoon cinnamon

Combine the rice and water in a saucepan. Bring to a simmer. Simmer for 15 minutes; drain. Combine the salt, sugar, cardamom, milk, eggs, almond extract and cinnamon in a bowl and mix well. Stir in the cooked rice.

Pour the pudding into a buttered 3-quart baking dish. Bake at 300 degrees for 1 hour, stirring after 30 minutes.

You may serve this warm or cold. It is great with port and fruit. Keep in mind that only Swedish kids like cardamom. SERVES 6 TO 8

PINEAPPLE CRISP

1/4 cup (1/2 stick) butter
1 (1-pound) package brown sugar
2 cans crushed pineapple
1 package yellow cake mix
Mazola butter-flavor nonstick cooking spray
1/4 cup (1/2 stick) butter
1/2 cup water

Place 1/4 cup butter in a 9×12-inch nonstick baking pan. Place in a 350-degree oven. Remove the pan after 2 to 5 minutes or when the butter is melted. Tilt the pan to coat the bottom evenly with the butter.

Pour the brown sugar over the melted butter. Press down and evenly distribute over the bottom of the pan. Pour the undrained crushed pineapple evenly over the brown sugar. Pour the cake mix evenly over the pineapple and press down gently. Spray the cake mix layer with Pam.

Cut 1/4 cup butter into thin slices. Arrange over the cake mix layer. Sprinkle the water over the top. Bake at 350 degrees for 1 hour. Let stand until cool. Chill, covered, until ready to serve. SERVES 12 TO 15

TIP: Feel free to substitute any fruit filling for the pineapple. If you use cherry pie filling, increase the water by 1/4 cup as the filling is thick.

CINNAMON PEACH CRUMBLE

This is great as a weeknight dessert, or as an addition to a brunch menu, or even as a way to soften your explanation of how you drove out of the garage with the door still closed. Warm, fruity, cinnamon-tinged food is just encouraging in its own right. Feel free to be manipulative with baked goods!!!!

2 eggs
1/2 cup sugar
2 teaspoons vanilla extract
2 teaspoons cinnamon
2 tablespoons butter, melted
1 cup self-rising flour
Canned sliced peaches, drained
1/2 cup chopped pecans
1/2 cup packed brown sugar
2 pats of butter

Combine the eggs, sugar, vanilla, cinnamon and 2 tablespoons butter in a large bowl and mix well. Sift in the flour and mix with a fork.

Pour half the batter into a buttered square nonstick baking pan. Cover the batter with the peaches. Sprinkle the pecans and brown sugar evenly over the batter. Dot with 2 pats of butter.

Drizzle the remaining batter unevenly over the layers, allowing some of the pecans to be shown. Bake at 325 degrees for 35 to 45 minutes. SERVES 6 TO 9

POACHED PEAR CHEESECAKE

16 ounces Philadelphia cream cheese, softened
2 eggs
1 cup sour cream
1 teaspoon vanilla extract
1 teaspoon cinnamon
1/4 teaspoon nutmeg
2 tablespoons cinnamon
1/4 cup sugar
6 canned pear halves
1 (10-inch) graham cracker pie shell

Beat the cream cheese, eggs, sour cream, vanilla, 1 teaspoon cinnamon and nutmeg in a mixing bowl until smooth.

Combine 2 tablespoons cinnamon and the sugar in a shallow dish and mix well. Pat the pear halves dry and cut lengthwise into slices. Arrange the pear slices in a spoke pattern over the bottom of the pie shell. Sprinkle half the cinnamon-sugar mixture over the pear slices.

Pour the batter over the pears. Sprinkle the remaining cinnamon-sugar mixture over the top of the batter. Bake at 350 degrees for 45 minutes. Let stand until room temperature. Chill, covered, until ready to serve.

You may substitute a pie shell made from sugar cookie dough for the graham cracker pie shell. SERVES 6 TO 8

TIP: The eggs must be fully cooked, so bake for at least 20 minutes. The depth and size of your pan may vary, so feel free to add or delete extra pears to make it work in your selected pan.

EASY CHOCOLATE-COVERED CHEESECAKE

3/4 cup milk
2 teaspoons vanilla extract
2 medium eggs
1 cup sugar
1/2 cup Bisquick or pancake flour
16 ounces cream cheese, softened
3 Hershey's candy bars

Preheat the oven to 350 degrees. Beat the milk, vanilla, eggs, sugar and Bisquick in a mixing bowl until smooth. Add 8 ounces of the cream cheese and beat until smooth. Add the remaining 8 ounces cream cheese and beat until smooth. Pour the batter into a 9-inch pie plate sprayed with nonstick cooking spray. Bake for 45 minutes or until the center is risen.

Place the unwrapped candy bars in a single layer on top of the hot cheesecake. Let stand until softened. Spread the chocolate over the top of the cheesecake. Let stand until cool. Chill until ready to serve.

This is based on the cheese pie in the original Bisquick cookbook. SERVES 6

PRALINE BANANA CHEESECAKE

3/4 cup sugar
1/2 cup White Lily or King Arthur flour
1/2 cup sweetened condensed milk
2 teaspoons vanilla extract
16 ounces good quality cream cheese, softened
1 teaspoon cinnamon
1/2 cup packed brown sugar
3 bananas

Beat the sugar, flour, milk, vanilla, cream cheese and cinnamon in a mixing bowl. Pour into a buttered deep 91/2-inch pie plate.

Place the brown sugar in a shallow dish. Slice the bananas 3/4 inch thick. Roll the bananas in the brown sugar to coat. Arrange evenly distributed over the batter. Bake at 325 degrees for 45 minutes. SERVES 6

DULCE DE LECHE TOBAGO

This is a classic dessert around the world. It is very dense...not loose like a crème brûlée...so you can serve just a little with fresh fruit. This recipe makes use of sweetened condensed milk, which simplifies the process considerably.

2 (14-ounce) cans sweetened condensed milk
1/2 cup Captain Morgan's spiced rum
1/2 teaspoon vanilla extract
1/8 teaspoon allspice
1/8 teaspoon salt

Pour the milk into a 9-inch round baking pan. Cover loosely with foil. Place the pan in a brazier or Dutch oven that is at least 10 inches in diameter. Add enough water to the larger pan to come halfway up the side of the smaller pan. Bake at 425 degrees for 45 minutes. Reduce the temperature to 350 degrees. Bake for 1 hour. Let stand at room temperature for 1 1/2 hours; do not refrigerate.

Stir the caramelized milk briskly. Whisk in the rum, vanilla, allspice and salt. Chill, covered, for 8 to 12 hours. Cut into wedges. Serve with fresh pineapple. SERVES 8

BASIC FLAN (APRICOT)

1 cup apricot brandy
1/2 cup sugar
1 1/2 cups whipping cream
4 eggs

Preheat the oven to 325 degrees. Boil the brandy in a saucepan until reduced by half. Remove from the heat. Add the sugar and stir until dissolved. Pour into a 2-quart bowl.

Whisk the whipping cream into the brandy mixture briskly. Add the eggs and whisk briskly until fluffy.

For individual flans, divide the mixture evenly among 4 to 6 custard cups. Place the cups on a rimmed baking sheet. For a large flan, pour the mixture into a baking dish. Place the dish on a rimmed baking sheet. Add water to the baking sheet to a depth of 1/2 inch. Bake for 15 minutes or until set. Refrigerate until chilled.

Garnish the flan with fresh berries or vanilla yogurt spiced with brown sugar and cinnamon. SERVES 4 TO 6

NOTES: My favorite topping is to put shredded dried apricots in apricot brandy to soak it up. Or, you can boil them in a little water and use the liquid, which gets syrupy, too. This is considered very fancy, but it's not hard at all.

For a custard pie, pour the cream mixture into an 8-inch pie shell. As I said, this process is simply a procedure for you to modify at will.

Other alternatives...substitute 1 cup port or brandy for the apricot brandy and top with sautéed walnuts, or use 1 cup Chambord and top with raspberries, or 1 cup Frangelica topped with slivered almonds and chocolate chips. All delicious.

For a savory flan...(as in not sweet)...omit the sugar and add 1/2 teaspoon pepper and 1/2 teaspoon salt. Add 1 cup chicken broth in place of the liquors and top with sautéed mushrooms or onions. Use 1/2 cup Cognac combined with 1/2 cup water and top with pulled chicken and roasted chopped chestnuts.

You can pour this into a shallow 8-inch pie plate and make a quiche cooked with veggies, cooked meat, nuts, shrimp...whatever you can dream up! So, if you can just get the four-basic-step concept mastered into a comfortable process, you can make four different types of food and be wildly creative without taking another step until you are anxious to do so because of your fabulous secret!

CONDIMENTS, MARINADES AND SAUCES

The simple ideas and recipes in this section can bring a plain roast chicken to the brink of genius! Marinating an item or just adding a condiment of distinction to a tired menu can dramatically alter it visually and experientially...no other decision in the kitchen requires so little effort for such a great reward.

Brush a fryer with honey and then sprinkle it with curry powder. Place it on a bed of sliced onions before you place it in the oven to bake...now it's...**SANDALWOOD CHICKEN** with onion confit...and the onion confit cooks in the bottom of the pan while the chicken cooks. A juicy and flavorful condiment that helped your chicken stay moist in the process. Pork tenderloin marinated in soy sauce and honey served with thin chopped cabbage sautéed in toasted sesame oil becomes...**KOWLOON PORK LOIN** with sesame cabbage. Coat a flank steak with a purchased fajita rub. While it grills, mix a can of black beans, a can of corn, and a same size jar of salsa (in other words, equal parts), serve with lettuce, flour tortillas, and sour cream, then enjoy...**CARNE PRESIDENTE**!!!!!! Now you can play the name game! Remember, you can buy condiments ready to go to build your confidence, but you will find your rapidly transforming fruitful mind creating its own...eventually. Express yourself! Well and often.

If you have no idea what to buy for your first (or updated) marinating/ super saucing adventure, I suggest four products in the "spice exchange" line of imports from Figueroa Brothers in Louisiana (see Sources). These can be sauces or marinades, alone or combined with other ingredients. Most importantly, they have little or no oil, are very low in calories (like five to eighteen per tablespoon) and sodium, come in flat fridge- and pantry-friendly bottles, and are clever and full of flavor. Try "Mango Heat" (add a little Grand Marnier!). "Rosemary Chipotle" is fabulous on pork or chicken. "Jerk Sauce" makes plain oven-roasted chicken wings or breasts a vacation experience! "Dark Rum with Coconut and Pineapple" is vibrant, fruity, and could be a dipping sauce used in concert with any of the others at the same meal. Live a little!

NOTE: These are pretty hot (spicy) for kids or Anglos over fifty, but they represent great value because they are concentrated, so dilute to your heart's content!

CONTENTS

ARGENTINA CHIMICHURRI

Argentina Chimichurri is a spicy condiment to use as an alternative to horseradish for beef, but it is also excellent with grilled fish, shrimp, or vegetables. It has the consistency of pesto but quite a different BITE—not nearly as mellow or aromatic.

2 large bunches parsley, stems removed
2 tablespoons oil-packed minced garlic
1/8 lemon (peel, pith and all!)
1/2 cup extra-virgin olive oil
1/2 cup white vinegar
1/2 teaspoon red pepper flakes

Combine the parsley, garlic, lemon, olive oil, vinegar and red pepper flakes in a food processor. Process for 1 minute or until smooth; the mixture should be bright green.

Serve with beef, grilled fish, shrimp or vegetables. You may also add this to salad dressing or a favorite marinade. Have fun with it. MAKES 2 CUPS

PESTO LA COSTA

This is a refreshing and eye-catching fast blender sauce for cooked shrimp, chicken, or just-cooked pasta. For a truly summer finish, add two cups of chopped ripe tomatoes to the completed pesto.

1 cup packed fresh parsley leaves
1/4 cup extra-virgin olive oil
1 tablespoon oil-packed minced garlic
1 tablespoon capers
1 tablespoon lemon juice
1 teaspoon Dijon mustard
2 chicken or vegetable bouillon cubes

Combine the parsley, olive oil, garlic, capers, lemon juice, Dijon mustard and bouillon cubes in a food processor. Process until smooth. Combine with cooked shrimp, chicken or hot just-drained pasta to serve. MAKES 1 CUP

ITALIAN PEPPER RAGÙ

A ragù or ragout is a stew. Anything can be stewed, and stews exist by many names in many cultures. If you stew something until it disintegrates, it can be a soup or a sauce. This recipe can turn a plain broiled chicken breast into a wonderful, satisfying meal. A beginner could serve it with store-bought rotisserie chicken, rice, or pasta, adding a platter of exotic olives and a good bread, artfully presented. The spicy flavor of this long-cooked complement changes the whole meal.

1/4 cup extra-virgin olive oil
1 tablespoon oil-packed minced garlic
2 large onions, sliced
1 each red, green and yellow bell pepper, thinly sliced
2 tablespoons white balsamic vinegar
6 crushed leaves fresh rosemary, or
    1/4 teaspoon ground rosemary

Heat the olive oil in a 3-quart saucepan. Add the garlic, onions, bell peppers, vinegar and rosemary. Sauté for 30 minutes or until the vegetables are tender. Serve as a condiment with vegetables or as a bed for fish or meat. It is excellent warm, hot or cold! You may add raisins or a little orange peel and chopped peaches, and it's a chutney. MAKES 3 CUPS

MEDITERRANEAN SALSA VERDE

This is a great condiment for plain broiled fish or chicken. It can be added in equal parts to commercial salad dressing for a great "fresh" dressing. It can be mixed in equal parts with mayonnaise and used with leftover chicken to make a great chicken salad; serve with slabs of ripe tomato and bread with tapenade.

1/4 cup packed fresh parsley leaves
1 large garlic clove
1/2 small red onion
1/2 teaspoon Dijon mustard
Juice of 1 lemon
1/2 cup olive oil
Salt and freshly ground pepper to taste

Place the parsley in a food processor. Add the garlic and onion through the feeder tube, processing until minced and stopping once to scrape down the side of the bowl. Add the Dijon mustard and lemon juice. Add the olive oil gradually, processing until the mixture is coarsely puréed and scraping down the side of the bowl as needed. Season with salt and pepper. MAKES 1 CUP

DOWN WITH TARTAR SAUCE
(A NEW CONDIMENT FOR GRILLED FISH)

1 cup sour cream
Pinch each of salt and white pepper
1/2 teaspoon grated lemon zest
Chopped fresh parsley or chives to taste
1 (3-ounce) jar good quality black caviar

Combine the sour cream with the salt and white pepper in a small bowl. Add the lemon zest and parsley and mix well. Add the caviar and stir gently so as not to bruise the caviar. Serve with grilled fish. MAKES 1¼ CUPS

NANA RUTH'S GRILL CONDIMENT

Apply this all-purpose barbecue sauce to the meat after it is grilled; it's a lot less messy. Because it is cooked, it still has the mellow warmth you get from basting, but you don't burn the meat or lose the sauce during the grilling.

1/2 cup brewed coffee
1/2 cup catsup
1/4 cup white vinegar
3 tablespoons brown sugar
2 teaspoons oil-packed minced garlic

Combine the coffee, catsup, vinegar and brown sugar in a medium saucepan and mix well. Simmer over low heat for 10 minutes or longer. Serve warm over grilled meats. MAKES 1¼ CUPS

NOTE: To modify this recipe, substitute lemon juice for the vinegar and double the garlic. You can also add orange zest or Grand Marnier, or 1/4 cup soy sauce and 1/2 teaspoon ground ginger.

CRANBERRY SANDWICH POLISH

This is good to serve with leftover turkey at Thanksgiving or anytime.

1 cup Hellman's mayonnaise
1/2 cup canned whole cranberry sauce
Squeeze of lemon juice
1/2 teaspoon pepper

Combine the mayonnaise, cranberry sauce, lemon juice and pepper in a bowl and mix well. Use as a spread for turkey sandwiches. MAKES 1 1/2 CUPS

NOTE: To make mayonnaise with other flavors, for each cup of mayonnaise, you could add lemon or orange extract to taste;
(OR) 1/2 cup chopped stuffed olives;
(OR) 1/2 cup chopped black olives;
(OR) 1/2 cup chopped roasted red bell pepper.
You can also add 1/2 cup Heinz catsup and a tablespoon of relish for the Russian dressing used on deli sandwiches by the billion in New York.

UNIVERSAL MARINADE

1/4 cup extra-virgin olive oil or neutral safflower oil
1/2 cup lemon juice
1 tablespoon oil-packed minced garlic
1/2 teaspoon sugar
1/2 teaspoon each salt and pepper

Combine the olive oil, lemon juice, garlic, sugar, salt and pepper in a bowl and mix well. Use as a marinade for 3 to 5 pounds of pork, beef, chicken, fish or vegetables.
MAKES ABOUT 1 CUP

NOTE: From this very basic recipe, you can move in any direction you want!
You can add 1/2 cup bourbon and 1/2 cup packed brown sugar;
(OR) 1 cup catsup and 1 cup salsa;
(OR) 1/2 cup soy sauce and 1/2 cup pineapple juice;
(OR) 1/2 cup orange marmalade;
(OR) 1 (12-ounce) can apricot nectar and 1 tablespoon jerk seasoning;
(OR) 1 cup boiled cider and 1 tablespoon pepper.

ORIENTAL SESAME MARINADE

1/2 cup soy sauce
1/4 cup toasted sesame oil
1 tablespoon ground ginger, or 1 (1-inch) piece peeled gingerroot
1 tablespoon ground garlic, or 2 garlic cloves
1 teaspoon arrowroot

Combine the soy sauce, sesame oil, ginger, garlic and arrowroot in a blender. Process for 1 minute.

Marinate 3 to 5 pounds of meat in the refrigerator for 2 hours or longer. Bake, broil or grill the meat. MAKES ABOUT 1 CUP

NOTE: You can add 2 fresh peaches before blending to this for an entirely different taste. If you change the sesame oil to safflower oil, it's totally different also, with or without the peaches.

ASIAN FRAGRANCES

This versatile recipe can serve as an Asian stir-fry or basting sauce. It is also good as a marinade for meat or vegetables that are to be grilled, stir-fried, or broiled.

3 tablespoons soy sauce
1 teaspoon sugar
1 teaspoon five-spice powder
1 teaspoon oil-packed minced garlic
1 teaspoon vegetable oil
1 tablespoon peanut butter and/or
    3 tablespoons sherry, orange juice, Cognac or rice wine
1/2 teaspoon ground ginger (optional)
1/2 teaspoon pepper (optional)

Combine the soy sauce with the sugar, five-spice powder, garlic and oil in a bowl. Add the peanut butter and/or any of the other ingredients to create the taste you prefer. MAKES A VARIABLE AMOUNT

MARINADES

Marinades are made up of three components:

Acid, such as lemon juice, wine, yogurt, fruit juice, tomato juice, etc. (NOT vinegar, with the exception of sauerbraten)
A little oil
Flavors, such as dry or prepared mustard, sugar, herbs, puréed fruit, coconut, spices, etc.

You can also add a fourth item as a thickener if desired. One-half teaspoon cornstarch or arrowroot to 2 cups liquid will tighten a sauce and make it glossy. Too much will make it burn, however.

As you can see, the options are limitless! So, if you can stir, place meat in a bowl and turn on the broiler or oven, you're good to go!

You can revise the recipes in this book for at least 100 new combinations once you're comfortable with experimentation.

SEMI-SAUCES

Sauces have fallen out of favor in the last five years in favor of marinades, rubs, and exotic condiments. This is due to the fact that they are perceived as ALWAYS being fattening! Not necessarily so. Here is a double-duty trick to give you an excellent lunch one day and a classic sauce another! The options rely on flavor more than on fat and can even be good without the addition of carbohydrates like flour. The choice is yours—experiment.

1 quart (4 cups) water
4 chicken bouillon cubes
2 large ribs celery, cut into halves
1 whole potato, peeled and chopped
1 carrot, peeled and chopped
1 bay leaf

Combine the water, chicken bouillon cubes, celery, potato, carrot and bay leaf in a 2-quart saucepan. Bring to a simmer. Go about your business for an hour or two while this simmers and makes your abode smell like heaven! Strain the stock, discarding the vegetables, or purée the vegetables and return them to the stock. Simmer the stock until it is reduced to 2 cups, or 4 cups if you added the puréed vegetables; it will be rich and complex. MAKES 2 CUPS

NOTE: Thicken the stock to serve as a light chicken jus; add a little wine and arrowroot for a wine sauce; or add 1/2 cup heavy cream for a cream gravy! All are excellent.

This recipe will work for beef, fish, or vegetarian sauces just by changing the original broth! Bases and bouillon come in many flavors, including onion, lobster, turkey, pork, mushroom, etc.

MAIN
COURSES

Growing up, I had the luxury of having a stay-at-home mom. She could focus on cooking skills, designing and stitching beautiful clothes, gardening, and creating a generally artful home. My own children, and those of most parents today, have working moms. But they still need to be fed! Eating out takes a LOT of time and money, and if you're enjoying that food, and having a **good** time, you're doing two things at once, so it's OK. In our ever-expanding and over-committed lives, doing two things at once is necessary for us to achieve some measure of success. When you can cook quickly and effortlessly at home, you can also talk to your mom or your grandmother, sing along with the video that your two-year-old is watching, or help with spelling drills. KEEP THIS IN MIND—when thinking in the direction of double accomplishment, it will come, and with it, a little more time will be freed up. Use it to have some FUN...it is excellent for your health and in very short supply in most adult lives!!!!

Consider this: Whenever you are grilling steaks on Sunday night, cook a few chicken breasts (or salmon, or anything grillable) for Tuesday. There are a lot of great ways to re-finish these meats into a great meal in five minutes. Or you could just cook more of the meat to be left, but two things happen: (1) you may eat it today, or (2) it may seem like leftovers, not the preparation of Step One in Tuesday's meal. This is investment cooking. Baja Wraps are a perfect example of how this can work (pages 83 and 84).

Try not to think of main courses as always being entrées comprised of a starch, a vegetable, and a meat, fish, or chicken. A broiled fillet of fish hot off the grill or broiler can be placed atop individual plates of salad with assorted raw vegetables in their midst and a dressing perfect for both. Leftover spaghetti can be paired with a rotisserie chicken and Italian Pepper Ragù (page 69) on a mess of quickly sautéed fresh zucchini or spinach. That same leftover spaghetti and sauce could be layered in a loaf pan alternating cheese with eggplant, zucchini, and spinach, baked like lasagna, and served alone.

CONTENTS

EASIEST-EVER POT ROAST

This pot roast recipe mirrors the "cook while you are gone" concept I discussed in the introduction. It is so easy you can't believe it can be that good...but it is. I have even done it in the bottom half of the broiler pan (on vacation) when I didn't have a roasting pan and it was PERFECT! I like to put a half-dozen big fat peeled carrots cut into chunks around it so they cook at the same time. The leftovers are really great for fajitas or hot beef sandwiches, or just stirred into mushroom risotto, etc.

4 cups water
1 envelope onion soup mix
1 (4-pound) 2-inch blade-cut chuck pot roast

Combine the water and onion soup mix in the bottom of a 9×12-inch roasting pan. Place the roast in the pan. Bake the roast at 300 degrees for 2 1/2 hours; at 250 degrees for 3 1/4 hours; or at 475 degrees for 30 minutes and then 200 degrees for 4 1/2 hours. SERVES 8 TO 12

NOTE: If you want to go Italian...replace 1 cup of water with 2 cups of red wine and you can make a "spuntino," which translates as "overcooked meat" or "potted meat." From the Piedmont to Reggio-Emilia in Italy's center, this is a "stracotto" when accompanied by pastina or orzo on the side and served with sautéed fresh spinach with a little fresh garlic and, of course, excellent bread to sop up the great jus! Serve with mashed potatoes and green beans, if you're traditional.

THINK-AHEAD BAJA WRAPS

Why think ahead? Because when you have that pre-cooked chicken or beef in the fridge from the last time you grilled or broiled, you are twenty minutes ahead on dinner tonight, you have less heat in the summer, and you have less cleanup.

Beef or chicken
Dry fajita seasoning, such as fajita seasoning from
   Coyote Country Seasoning Company
6-inch flour tortillas
1 bottle Kraft ranch salad dressing
1 jar salsa
1 bag shredded lettuce

The day you cook, moisten the beef and place on a platter wet. Sprinkle generously with fajita seasoning, turning over several times and covering completely. Wrap in plastic wrap and chill until ready to grill.

Unwrap the beef. Grill over hot coals until cooked to the desired degree of doneness. Slice the beef into 1/2-inch strips. Chill, covered, until ready to serve.

On the day you eat, place the beef on a microwave-safe plate. Heat on High for 2 to 3 minutes or until warm. Place the tortillas on a microwave-safe plate. Heat on High for 1 minute or until warm.

Serve the beef and tortillas with the ranch salad dressing, salsa and lettuce. The assembly, cutting and heating should take approximately 10 minutes. Sit down, wrap as you eat and visit! MAKES VARIABLE SERVINGS

NOTE: The recipe on the facing page can, of course, be prepared for same-day consumption, and the accompaniments could be extended to include corn, black beans, cheese, freshly diced tomatoes, and many other options. This recipe (menu), however, is very fully flavored and surprisingly complete without any other time added.

This same meat preparation could be served with a sandwich polish (see Condiments chapter) on store-bought bread with good beer for a mid-week night with friends when sports are on TV. This carries the same ten-minute preparation time and is much better than ordering a pizza.

Most of the recipes in here can be used with already cooked products and finished quickly into a different meal.

MAXIMUM THREE-MINUTE MEAT LOAF

2 pounds lean ground beef
1/4 cup water
1 envelope onion soup mix
1 egg

Combine the ground beef, water, onion soup mix and egg in a bowl and mix well. Shape into a loaf and place in a 9-inch square baking pan. Bake in a preheated 350-degree oven for 35 minutes. SERVES 6 TO 8

NOTE: You may double this and increase the cooking time to 52 minutes and the pan size to 9×13 inches.

JUICY ONION BURGERS

1 envelope Lipton Beefy Onion soup mix
2 1/2 pounds lean ground chuck
3 tablespoons water
3 tablespoons catsup
1 egg

Combine the soup mix, ground chuck, water, catsup and egg in a bowl and mix well. Shape into patties.

Place the patties on a rack in a broiler pan. Broil to the desired degree of doneness, turning once. You may place on a grill rack and grill to the desired degree of doneness, turning once. SERVES 8 TO 12

NOTE: You may substitute ground turkey for the ground chuck, omit the water and add 1 tablespoon of bread crumbs.

CARNITAS

1 (1-pound) partially frozen pork tenderloin
1 package fajita seasoning mix
1 onion, thinly sliced
1 green bell pepper, thinly sliced
Extra-virgin olive oil
1/2 bottle beer

Cut the pork into 1/2-inch circles. Place the seasoning in a plastic bag. Add the pork and shake to coat. Sauté the onion and bell pepper in olive oil in a skillet for 3 minutes. Add the pork. Cook for 5 minutes, adding a splash of beer if the pork sticks or begins to burn. You may substitute weak grapefruit juice for the beer.
SERVES 4

AUTUMN SWISS SKILLET DINNER

1 (8-ounce) package broad egg noodles
2 cups split brussels sprouts, or 12 ounces frozen brussels sprouts
2 tablespoons butter
2 large onions, sliced
1/2 red bell pepper, sliced
2 teaspoons brown sugar
2 teaspoons cider vinegar
1/3 cup canned chicken broth
1 cup corn, or 1 small can corn
4 smoked bone-in pork chops

Cook the noodles using the package directions; drain. Bring enough water to cover the brussels sprouts to a boil in a saucepan. Add the brussels sprouts. Cook until tender-crisp; drain.

Heat the butter in a 3- to 5-quart Dutch oven until melted. Add the onions. Sauté for 10 minutes or until tender. Add the bell pepper, brown sugar and vinegar. Cook for 5 minutes, stirring occasionally.

Add the chicken broth to the onion mixture. Cook until the mixture thickens. Add the corn, pork chops, cooked noodles and cooked brussels sprouts. Bring to a boil. Remove from the heat. Let stand for 5 minutes.

Serve from the pan or arrange on a platter. SERVES 4

FRESH HAM HAVANA

1 (3-pound) lean boneless pork roast, tied
3 tablespoons oil-packed minced garlic
1 tablespoon oregano
1 tablespoon cinnamon
Juice of 1 orange
Juice of 1 lime
1 tablespoon cider vinegar
2 tablespoons olive oil
2 tablespoons catsup

Place the pork in a sealable plastic bag. Combine the garlic, oregano, cinnamon, orange juice, lime juice, vinegar, olive oil and catsup in a bowl and mix well.

Pour the marinade over the pork and seal the bag. Turn to coat the pork. Marinate in the refrigerator for up to 36 hours, turning and piercing the pork every 6 to 8 hours.

Drain the pork and discard the marinade. Place in a roasting pan. Roast at 325 degrees for 2 hours or to 175 degrees on a meat thermometer. SERVES 8 TO 12

NOTE: I like to serve this with corn and potato hash and a microwaved green vegetable or a salad. The hash can be made in the oven during the last hour at the same time the meat is roasting (I am so lazy!). Toss four diced potatoes (I don't even peel them), one drained 8- to 12-ounce can of black beans, one 12-ounce bag of frozen corn, 1/2 cup of salsa and 1/2 teaspoon of salt together on a baking sheet or shallow roasting pan. Spread evenly and bake until the roast is ready!

CREAMY VEAL ROAST

1 (2-pound) blade-cut veal chuck roast
2 cups buttermilk
1 tablespoon oil-packed minced garlic
1 teaspoon thyme
2 potatoes, cut into quarters
4 carrots, peeled and cut into halves
2 onions, sliced
2 celery ribs, chopped
2 chicken bouillon cubes
1 cup water

Place the veal in a sealable plastic bag. Pour the buttermilk over the veal. Add the garlic and thyme. Seal the bag and tilt to coat the veal. Marinate in the refrigerator for 48 hours, turning occasionally. Drain, discarding the marinade.

Place the veal in a roasting pan. Add the potatoes, carrots, onions, celery, chicken bouillon cubes and water. Bake at 350 degrees for 2 hours. Serve the veal with the pan juices and green peas. SERVES 6 TO 8

GRILLED CHICKEN PROVENÇALE

Good for a group!

3 cups thickly sliced plum tomatoes
3 cups drained artichoke hearts
1 cup coarsely chopped fennel
2 teaspoons oil-packed minced garlic
1/2 cup crushed niçoise olives
1/4 cup olive oil
Leaves from a 2-inch piece of rosemary, or 1/2 teaspoon dried rosemary
2 tablespoons chopped fresh thyme, or 1/2 teaspoon dried thyme
1 cup strong chicken broth
8 shallots, peeled and crushed
3 to 5 pounds cooked chicken breast strips, tenderloin or drumsticks

Toss the tomatoes, artichoke hearts, fennel, garlic, olives, olive oil, rosemary, thyme, chicken broth and shallots together in a large roasting pan. Bake at 375 degrees for 1 hour.

Add the chicken to the vegetables and stir to combine. Bake at 325 degrees for 30 minutes.

You may substitute the meat of 2 rotisseried chickens for the 3 to 5 pounds cooked chicken. SERVES 10

NOTE: Use these options and expand. This is very French/Mediterranean, fragrant, and richly rewarding. Once you have prepped the veggies, it makes itself.

TANDOORI-STYLE CURRY ROASTED CHICKEN

¹/₂ cup honey
1 teaspoon paprika
1 teaspoon curry powder or garam masala
2 frying chickens, or 1 Purdue Sunday Best Roaster
8 to 10 prunes

Combine the honey, paprika and curry powder in a bowl and mix well. Set a small amount aside. Brush over the chickens. Place the chickens in a baking pan. Arrange the prunes around the chickens.

Bake the chickens at 400 degrees for 20 minutes. Reduce the temperature to 250 degrees. Bake for an additional 45 minutes. Brush with the reserved honey mixture.

Serve with hot or cold Chai (spicy tea) for a transporting experience. SERVES 6 TO 8

NOTE: I once soaked two fryers in unsweetened tea overnight and then did this procedure. They were quite exotic and wonderful! Serve either style with Jewel Box Rice for a standing ovation from beaming eaters.

A garam masala is like a "house blend" of spices someone specific likes. The marketplace is filled with different kinds of red, green, and gold curries and curry pastes as well as garam masalas. If you use a different one every time, this will never be the same dish! When you love one type in particular, then it becomes your signature curry.

HARVEST CHICKEN

4 (6- to 8-ounce) chicken breasts
2 cups Ocean Spray cranapple juice
1 Granny Smith apple, peeled and sliced
1 cup water
2 chicken bouillon cubes
Pinch of cinnamon
1/4 cup bourbon or applejack
1 teaspoon white vinegar
1 teaspoon honey

Spray a heavy bottomed Dutch oven with butter-flavor Pam. Add the chicken. Cook over low heat for 5 to 15 minutes or until brown; this adds extra flavor.

Add the juice, apple, water, chicken bouillon cubes, cinnamon, bourbon, vinegar and honey to the chicken. Bake at 375 degrees for 40 minutes.

You may substitute 2 tablespoons melted butter for the Pam. SERVES 4

NOTE: This will make the whole house smell like fall. I make it the first night it is rational to make a fire without turning on the air conditioning. We live in the south, so at my house, we make a big deal about enhancing the seasonal changes we do experience.

ROMANO DIJON CHICKEN

Recipe compliments of Stephen Kori, Atlanta, Georgia.

4 boneless chicken breasts
1/2 cup (1 stick) butter
2 tablespoons Dijon mustard
1/2 teaspoon tarragon (optional)
Pepper to taste
1 cup (about) Italian or plain bread crumbs
1 cup (4 ounces) grated Romano cheese

Slice each chicken breast lengthwise into 2 or 3 thin strips.

Heat the butter in a small saucepan until melted. Whisk in the Dijon mustard, tarragon and pepper. Combine the bread crumbs and cheese in a bag.

Dip a chicken strip in the butter mixture and then roll in the bread crumb mixture. Place on a baking sheet. Repeat with the remaining chicken strips. Bake at 375 degrees for 30 minutes or until cooked through. SERVES 4

SNAPPER PROVENÇAL

One-dish dinners, especially when the dish itself goes into the dishwasher with no stove-top cleanup, really encourage cooking. This really healthy, wonderfully satisfying meal with just the addition of store-bought good quality bread and a nice Fumé Blanc is more like a restaurant meal. Assemble, heat, eat!

6 (4-ounce) fresh snapper fillets
Pepper to taste
1 tomato, chopped
4 small zucchini (courgettes), cut into 1/4- to 1/2-inch-thick slices, or
    an equivalent amount of carrots or celery
1/2 teaspoon oil-packed minced garlic
Butter
1 1/2 tablespoons chicken bouillon granules

Sprinkle the fillets on both sides with pepper. Spray a 9-inch square baking dish with nonstick cooking spray or butter generously. Arrange 3 fillets over the bottom; the fillets will overlap slightly.

Layer the tomato, zucchini, garlic and remaining 3 fillets over the fillets. Dab small amounts of butter over the fillets. Sprinkle the bouillon granules over the top. Cover with foil. Bake at 350 degrees for 25 minutes. Let stand for 5 minutes. SERVES 6

BAKED FISH VARIATIONS: Place the fillets in a baking dish. Microwave carrots, onions and celery until half cooked and very hot. Layer over the fish. Spoon Alfredo sauce over the layers. Bake for 35 minutes. Serve over linguini.

Place the fillets in a baking dish. Layer chopped fresh tomatoes, red bell peppers, green bell peppers, yellow bell peppers, chopped onions and cooked chorizo sausage over the fillets. Serve with warm flour tortillas, fresh salsa and margaritas. Or spoon the fish mixture into flour tortillas at the table and top with some sour cream (Baja Fajita Style).

Place the fillets in a baking dish. Combine 1/4 cup soy sauce and 2 tablespoons sesame oil. Layer bean sprouts, chopped onions, snow peas, chopped carrots and fresh spinach leaves over the fillets. Splash liberally with the soy sauce mixture. Serve with rice, plum wine, orange slices and fortune cookies.

Add 8 ounces uncooked, peeled, deveined medium shrimp to any recipe as the middle layer and increase the cooking time by 15 minutes.

Pour 1/2 jar Prego spaghetti sauce over uncooked Snapper Provençal. Sprinkle with grated Parmesan cheese. Increase the cooking time by 15 minutes.

TIP: If snapper is not available, sea bass or sole will work, but you need to add bread crumbs to the vegetable mix and add a little more cooking time to accommodate the extra moisture from the "wetter" fish. This is also true if you substitute frozen cod or other frozen white-fleshed fish. Meaty fish like salmon or swordfish do not work for this preparation.

PIZZA PIZZAZZ

The concept of pizza in Italy is 2,500 years old but did not include tomatoes until Columbus brought them to Campania on his triumphant return from the Americas. So, pizza as we think of it is a nineteenth-century evolution. The point is it is a procedure like making a sandwich and thus has a million possibilities. I have found I can buy dough balls from Italian restaurants or grocery stores all over the world. So can you! Dough already rolled out and ready to top is also available from your grocer's freezer. In France, they call it Pissaladière. So, once you have made a pizza, you can do that, too!

1/4 **cup cornmeal**
1/4 **cup flour**
1/4 **teaspoon salt**
1 **dough ball**
Extra-virgin olive oil

Combine the cornmeal, flour and salt in a bowl and mix well. Sprinkle 2 tablespoons of the cornmeal mixture on a work surface. Stretch and press the dough out until it is about the size of a pizza pan, sprinkling additional cornmeal mixture on the work surface as needed.

Coat a pizza pan with olive oil. Place the dough in the pan. Pinch the edges if they hang over the side. Brush the exposed dough with olive oil. Set aside.
SERVES 2 TO 4

PIZZA OF NAPOLI
Thinly sliced tomatoes
Buffalo mozzarella slices
Chopped or whole fresh basil leaves
Salt to taste

Arrange the tomatoes, mozzarella and basil over the dough. Sprinkle with salt. Bake at 375 degrees for 20 minutes.

PIZZA OF PROVENCE

1 large sweet onion, cut into thin circles
1 teaspoon oil-packed minced garlic
2 teaspoons extra-virgin olive oil
1/2 cup coarsely chopped niçoise olives (do not substitute)
1/2 cup chopped tomato
Sea salt to taste
Pepper to taste

Combine the onion, garlic, olive oil and olives in a microwave-safe bowl and toss to combine. Microwave for 2 minutes. Let stand for 2 minutes. Arrange evenly over the dough. Sprinkle the tomato, sea salt and pepper over the onion mixture. Bake at 375 degrees for 20 minutes.

PIZZA OF CALABRIA

Chopped tomato
Flaked tuna
Chopped hard-cooked eggs
Capers
Lemon juice
Grated Parmesan cheese

Sprinkle the tomato, tuna, eggs, capers, lemon juice and cheese over the dough. Bake at 375 degrees for 20 minutes.

TIP: Pizza can be a main course or an accompaniment with just cheese and garlic. You can add herbs to the dough if you want to get fancy. Start with where you feel comfortable, then branch out. It is what they have been doing in Campania for at least 2,500 years!

LINGUINI WITH CLAM SAUCE

1 (12-ounce) package durum or semolina linguini
1 tablespoon oil-packed minced garlic
1 tablespoon extra-virgin olive oil
Pinch of white pepper
1 can clams, drained
1/4 cup dry white wine
2 cups water
2 chicken bouillon cubes
2 tablespoons cornstarch
1/2 cup warm heavy cream
1/4 cup (1 ounce) grated Parmesan cheese

Prepare the linguini according to the package directions. Drain and place on a warm serving platter.

Heat the garlic, olive oil and white pepper in a large heavy skillet. Add the clams and cook for 1 minute. Add the wine, water and chicken bouillon cubes. Cook for 3 minutes, stirring occasionally.

Combine the cornstarch and warm cream in a small bowl and mix well. Stir in the cheese.

Bring the clam mixture to a boil. Remove from the heat and stir in the cream mixture. Cook until the mixture begins to steam.

Pour the clam sauce over the pasta. Garnish with chopped chives. SERVES 4

RIVIERA SHRIMP

3 tablespoons extra-virgin olive oil
3 tablespoons Champagne vinegar or white wine vinegar
2 teaspoons Dijon mustard
1/2 teaspoon oil-packed minced garlic
1 tablespoon sugar
1 (2×2-inch) piece orange peel
1/4 cup chardonnay
1 green onion
2 pounds deveined peeled cooked large shrimp
3 mangoes, peeled and chopped
Coarsely ground pepper

Combine the olive oil, vinegar, Dijon mustard, garlic, sugar, orange peel and chardonnay in a blender. Process on High for 1 minute.

Cut the green part of the onion diagonally into 1/2-inch pieces. Combine the green onion pieces, shrimp, mangoes and sauce artfully in a serving dish. Sprinkle with pepper. Chill until ready to serve. SERVES 6 TO 8

VARIATION: Substitute corn and black beans for the mangoes and cilantro for the orange peel and omit the chardonnay.

SUMMER CITRUS SHRIMP

Cold shrimp is almost always appealing, but outdoor service in the heat can quickly make them "fishy." To correct that instantly...

1 pound deveined peeled cooked shrimp
2 cups pasteurized orange juice

Marinate the shrimp in the orange juice in a bowl in the refrigerator for up to 8 hours; do not marinate for more than 8 hours or the shrimp will be tough. The acids in the orange juice help to sterilize the surface and the sweetness is wonderful. Drain and discard the juice. Serve the shrimp with a wonderful sauce. My friend Marine McKee thinks this is the best-kept secret ever! SERVES 4

JAPANESE-STYLE SPRING VEGETABLE BOWL

4 cups water
2 packages chicken ramen noodles or similar organic noodle soup mix
1 tablespoon toasted sesame oil
1 tablespoon chopped gingerroot, or 1/4 teaspoon ginger powder
1 tablespoon soy sauce
1 carrot, peeled and shredded into thin circles
1 cup shredded bok choy (about 1 small head)
1/2 cup snow peas, cut in angles and tipped
1 cup chopped chicken

Bring the water to a boil in a 3-quart saucepan. Add the seasoning packets from the soup mixes. Add the next 6 ingredients. Bring to a boil. Add the noodles to the mixture. Simmer until soft. Add the chicken. Serve immediately. SERVES 4

NOTE: Modify additions to suit those you are serving—broccoli, shrimp, mushrooms, tomatoes, peas, onions, ground pork made into meatballs, clams, tofu, leftover salmon or swordfish...you get it.

TUSCAN BREAD SALAD

This is a summer entrée or lunch in hill towns all over Italy. It is filling and refreshing at the same time.

6 ripe tomatoes, chopped
2 cucumbers, peeled and chopped
1/2 bunch chives, chopped
1 red onion, finely chopped
1/2 cup finely torn fresh basil leaves
1/4 cup extra-virgin olive oil
1/2 cup good strong red wine vinegar
1/2 teaspoon salt
1/2 teaspoon pepper
1/2 teaspoon oil-packed minced garlic
1 (1-pound) loaf day-old Italian bread, torn into 1-inch chunks

Combine the tomatoes, cucumbers, chives, onion, basil, olive oil, vinegar, salt, pepper and garlic in a bowl and mix well. Add the bread and toss to combine. Chill the salad for 15 minutes. Toss and serve.

NOTE: In several cultures, old bread is used creatively to thicken via bread crumbs or to stretch out small amounts of fresh food like the fat crouton in French Onion Soup. In Italy, they layer old sliced bread (in an oven-safe terrine or crock) with squab (small yields of meat) and minced fresh vegetables, then cover it with boiling stock and put it in the oven for 30 minutes so the stock can be absorbed into a very wet casserole called "sopa cauda." Be resourceful—use everything!

SOUPS AND SIDES

*I have heard people say things like, "Oh, making a galantine of turkey and roasted red peppers is easy and fun...the creative process is so enriching!" Well, guess what? The same can be said for **routine brain surgery**...and with a million dollars in equipment and six assistants, it **IS** easy! Faced with the prospect of "easily making pasta" for the first time, it is appropriate for you to feel you need these same resources...and anyone would rather go out faced with that. Nothing is fun...when you can't do it! Conversely, it **is** easy to enjoy almost ANYTHING one does well. So, let's put to rest any guilt you feel over your wary attitude toward effortless cooking—or brain surgery!*

This book is about success without intimidation or maybe even earnest effort, because when you throw a few things together and enjoy it, your skills and your style will grow very quickly, as will your interest— not because of commitment, but because of success!

Soups and sides are a place to try your hand. On a night when you're going to Boston Market for a chicken, toss together an asparagus gratin and a plate of sliced ripe tomatoes. The gratin will finish in the time you pour the wine and grab the plates. What a very different dinner it will be. And if somehow you burn it or drop it...SO WHAT? You still have enough to eat.

Soup is a meal in a bowl. It can be the most comforting food on Earth. Whenever anything is wrong with anyone, I make them soup. An act of simple kindness can actually help in almost any situation.

CONTENTS

CREAM OF ARTICHOKE SOUP

To serve this soup as an entrée, you can add chopped leftover cooked chicken, chopped fresh spinach, cooked rice, or small cooked pasta. Season with a pinch of nutmeg and a liberal sprinkle of grated Parmesan cheese.

1 (10-ounce) package frozen artichoke hearts
2 cups half-and-half
2 chicken bouillon cubes
2 teaspoons dry sherry
1/2 teaspoon pepper

Combine the artichoke hearts, half-and-half, chicken bouillon cubes, sherry and pepper in a blender and process until smooth.

Pour into a saucepan and cook over medium heat just until heated through. Ladle into soup bowls. SERVES 4

For Smooth Mushroom Soup, substitute cleaned fresh mushrooms for the artichokes and process as above. Pour into a saucepan and cook until steamy. Cook for 5 minutes longer in case there are any bacteria remaining on the mushrooms—and you can assume there are.

For Chunky Mushroom Soup, sauté an additional 8 ounces of sliced mushrooms in 1 to 2 tablespoons of butter in a skillet. Add to the processed mushroom mixture and prepare as above.

THAI ONE ON—AN EXOTIC CARROT SOUP

2 pounds cooked carrots or frozen carrots
4 chicken bouillon cubes
2 cups unsweetened coconut milk
   (in the ethnic food section of the market)
2 cups water
2 teaspoons sesame oil
1 tablespoon oil-packed minced garlic
2 teaspoons onion powder
1 teaspoon ground ginger
Chili powder

Microwave the carrots using the package directions if using frozen carrots. Combine the carrots with the bouillon cubes in a food processor and process until smooth. Pour into a 4-quart saucepan.

Add the coconut milk, water, sesame oil, garlic, onion powder and ginger. Cook until heated through. Ladle into soup bowls.

Garnish with a sprinkle of chili powder and serve with pita bread. You may also enjoy serving this with chips, fruited salsa and a salad. SERVES 8

POTAGE NIVERNAISE—WONDERFUL WINTER SOUP OF CARROTS AND POTATOES

1 pound cooked carrots
1 pound mashed cooked potatoes
2 cups milk
1 onion, chopped (optional)
4 chicken bouillon cubes
2 tablespoons Cognac or other brandy (optional)
Pinch of nutmeg

Mash the carrots and potatoes in a medium stockpot until smooth. Add the milk, onion, chicken bouillon cubes, Cognac and nutmeg and mix well. Simmer over low heat just until the onion is tender. Ladle into soup bowls. SERVES 8

SUMMER CUCUMBER SOUP

This is a very popular soup in the Balkans...refreshing and filling!

1 cup each yogurt and sour cream
1 cup chopped peeled cucumber, about 2 medium cucumbers
1 teaspoon oil-packed minced garlic
2 tablespoons chopped fresh dill, or to taste
1 teaspoon pepper

Combine the yogurt, sour cream, cucumber, garlic, dill and pepper in a blender or food processor. Process until smooth. Chill in the refrigerator. Pour into soup bowls and garnish with paprika. SERVES 4

TIP: Serve Summer Cucumber Soup with turkey sandwiches made with roasted bell peppers on good French bread.

HUMITAS

This is a well-seasoned corn stew—like a Spanish version of Brunswick stew. It's not a soup, not a side dish, but it hovers in the world between. I like it.

1/2 cup chopped green onions
1/2 cup chopped red bell pepper
1/4 cup (1/2 stick) butter
6 cups frozen corn, thawed
3 eggs
1/2 cup milk
1/2 teaspoon pepper
1/2 cup (2 ounces) grated strong Parmesan cheese

Sauté the green onions and red bell pepper in the butter in a 4-quart saucepan.

Combine the corn, eggs, milk and pepper in a blender or food processor. Process for 30 to 45 seconds or until smooth. Add to the saucepan.

Cook for 10 minutes or until bubbly. Add the cheese and stir until the cheese melts. You can serve this as a main course with a good bread or a salad, chips and salsa.

SERVES 8

SUPER-FAST TRADITIONAL CHILI

If you are really in a hurry, you can make this with just salsa, beans, beef, and a pinch of salt!

1 pound lean ground beef
1 onion, chopped
1 teaspoon oil-packed minced garlic
1 beef bouillon cube
1 teaspoon pepper
1 (16-ounce) can pinto beans or mixed chili beans, drained and rinsed
1 (12-ounce) jar salsa

Brown the ground beef in a 10-inch skillet for 3 minutes or until nearly cooked through, stirring until crumbly.

Add the onion, garlic, beef bouillon cube and pepper. Cook for 3 minutes, stirring frequently.

Add the beans and salsa. Cook for 5 minutes longer. Ladle into bowls. Garnish with dollops of sour cream and sprinkle with cumin. SERVES 4

VEGETARIAN CHILI

8 ounces dried black beans, rinsed and sorted
1 (12-ounce) can pinto beans, drained
1 (12-ounce) can red beans, drained
2 large onions, coarsely chopped
2 green bell peppers, seeded, cored and coarsely chopped
1 (28- to 32-ounce) can chopped juice-packed tomatoes
1 (4-ounce) can chopped jalapeños (optional—these are hot)
2 tablespoons oil-packed minced garlic
4 cups water
4 vegetable bouillon cubes
1/4 cup chili powder
2 tablespoons ground cumin (not whole cumin seed)
1 small can tomato paste
1 (12-ounce) can corn, drained
Ground pepper to taste

Combine the black beans with water to cover in a bowl. Let stand for 8 hours.

Drain the black beans and combine with the pinto beans, red beans, onions and bell peppers in a 6-quart stockpot. Add the undrained tomatoes, jalapeños, garlic, water, vegetable bouillon cubes, chili powder and cumin and mix well. Cook over low heat or bake at 300 degrees for 2 hours.

Stir in the tomato paste, corn and pepper. Cook just until heated through, stirring frequently. SERVES 8 TO 10

NOTE: If you aren't worried about scorching the chili, you can add all the ingredients at once. The tomato paste, however, makes it thicker, so if you wait, it is less likely to stick to the bottom of the pan as the chili cooks.

SPRINGTIME ARTICHOKES

Harvest time for California artichokes is in April and May. If you LOVE to eat them fresh, buy them then. Heavy artichokes are fresher than their more dehydrated counterparts. Like lots of vegetables, they convert their sugar to starch as they age, thus losing their flavor.

Fresh artichokes
Salt
Lemon juice
Butter or white balsamic vinegar and olive oil

Trim the bottoms of the artichokes so they will sit upright. Cut off and discard 1/4 of the tops. Place upside down in a steamer basket in a stainless steel or enamel stockpot. Add 2 1/3 to 3 inches of water. Add a pinch of salt and a squeeze of lemon. Steam for 35 to 40 minutes or until a leaf can be easily pulled from the artichoke.

Serve with melted butter if you're skinny or with white balsamic vinegar and a little olive oil if you're not.

TIP: Fresh artichokes sing or squeak when rubbed with the index finger. They grunt or thud if they are over the hill. This is not a good way to judge your neighbors or co-workers.

ASPARAGUS GRATIN

1 pound asparagus
1 egg
1/2 cup milk
3/4 cup (3 ounces) grated Parmesan cheese
Pepper to taste

Trim up to 4 inches from the bottoms of the asparagus spears. Place on a microwave-safe plate and add a small amount of water. Microwave on High for 2 minutes; drain.

Butter a baking dish large enough to hold twice as much asparagus. Arrange the asparagus loosely in the baking dish.

Combine the egg and milk in a mixing bowl and mix well. Stir in 1/2 cup of the cheese. Pour over the asparagus. Sprinkle with the remaining 1/4 cup cheese and sprinkle generously with pepper.

Bake at 450 degrees for 5 minutes. Reduce the oven temperature to 300 degrees and bake for 10 minutes or longer if you prefer the asparagus more tender. Do not overbrown.

Serve warm with French bread and a crisp white wine. It's great with tapenade and olives before a main course salad.

TIP: You may add a little Dijon mustard, wine, or garlic to the egg mixture if you want a zestier taste. If asparagus is expensive, you can stretch it to serve more with the addition of mushroom halves, 1/2 cup sautéed onion, or 1/2 cup thinly sliced leek bulb.

PICNIC-STYLE OLD-FASHIONED BAKED BEANS

This is a recipe from the 1940s that has been modified for today. It will serve a group of sixteen, but you may reduce the recipe by half for a smaller family.

2 (16-ounce) cans Great Northern beans
1 (16-ounce) can pinto beans
1 (16-ounce) can kidney beans
1 cup chopped onion
1 (4-ounce) jar real bacon bits, or 4 slices Canadian bacon, chopped
1 cup catsup
1 can cola
1/4 cup cider vinegar
1 teaspoon salt
1 teaspoon pepper

Combine the beans, onion and bacon bits in a large mixing bowl. Add the catsup, cola, vinegar, salt and pepper and mix well.

Spoon into a baking pan. Bake at 375 degrees for 1 to 1 1/2 hours or until bubbly. The beans will continue to thicken as they cool. SERVES 12 TO 18

NOTE: I must have a whole big onion sliced up in my beans, but you be the judge for yours.

BABY FRENCH BEAN SALAD

1 pound haricots verts
3 tablespoons extra-virgin olive oil
3 tablespoons Champagne vinegar or white wine vinegar
2 teaspoons Dijon mustard
1/2 teaspoon prepared chopped garlic
1/2 teaspoon sugar
Salt and pepper to taste

Trim the beans and combine with a small amount of water in a saucepan or steamer. Steam, covered, for 5 minutes; drain.

Combine the olive oil, vinegar, Dijon mustard, garlic and sugar in a bowl and whisk to mix well. Pour the olive oil mixture over the beans.

Add salt and pepper to taste and toss to coat well. Serve warm or chilled. SERVES 4

LEMON BROCCOLI

Recipe compliments of Stephen Kori, Atlanta, Georgia.

1 pound broccoli florets
   (from the packaged salad section of the market)
3 garlic cloves
Juice of 1 lemon
1 to 3 tablespoons extra-virgin olive oil
Salt and pepper to taste

Microwave the broccoli for about 4 minutes using the package directions; drain. Crush the garlic in a medium glass serving dish.

Add the lemon juice, olive oil, salt and pepper; whisk to mix well. Add the broccoli and toss to coat evenly. SERVES 4

NOTE: I like to microwave the finished dish for 2 minutes to blend the garlic flavor with the broccoli.

CORN SOUFFLÉ OR CORN PUDDING

We use this as a combination vegetarian entrée or wonderful side dish on buffets at the Metropolitan Club. By adding black beans, shredded Cheddar cheese, red and green bell peppers sautéed with onions, and chopped fresh tomatoes or salsa, it becomes a centerpiece food. It is wonderful, and you can also choose to add rice if you need a side dish for a grilled meat or fish dinner.

6 large eggs
3 cups half-and-half
1/2 teaspoon salt
1/2 teaspoon pepper
6 cups frozen corn, thawed

Combine the eggs, half-and-half, salt and pepper in a blender or food processor. Pulse 10 times for 2 seconds each or until well blended. Stir in 3 cups of the corn. Add the remaining 3 cups corn and any other ingredients you may choose, as we do.

Spoon into a baking pan sprayed with nonstick cooking spray. Bake at 375 degrees for 25 minutes. SERVES 6

You may add onion, peppers, tomatoes, Cheddar cheese, black beans or anything southwestern, or even turn it into an entrée.

NOTE: If you prefer to use fresh corn off the cob, reduce the half-and-half by 1/2 cup.

UNEXPECTED EGGPLANT

Americans cook less with eggplant than Europeans and Asians. Break out and try something your mom didn't cook—or at least most moms. If you are a recent convert, peel the eggplant with a potato peeler. If you already love eggplant, feel free to leave the peel on.

1 eggplant, 3 to 4 inches in diameter
1 teaspoon garlic powder
1 teaspoon onion powder
1 teaspoon salt
1 teaspoon pepper
Juice of 1 lemon, or 2 tablespoons lemon juice
2 tablespoons water
Mazola garlic-flavored cooking spray

Preheat the oven to 400 degrees.

Cut off and discard 1 inch from each end of the eggplant. Slice the eggplant into 1/2- to 3/4-inch circles.

Combine the garlic powder, onion powder, salt and pepper in a small bowl. Mix the lemon juice and water in a second small bowl.

Brush both sides of each eggplant slice with the lemon juice mixture and rub with the seasoning blend. Arrange on a nonstick baking sheet. Spray the slices with cooking spray.

Bake for 45 minutes. Serve with spaghetti sauce on the side. SERVES 4 TO 6

NOTE: You can layer this with leftover pasta, ricotta cheese, and spaghetti sauce in a nonstick round or oval baking dish and top with grated cheese. You can also alternate layers of eggplant between layers of ricotta cheese and freshly grated Parmesan cheese if you have no leftover pasta.

YORKSHIRE-STYLE MUSHROOM PUDDING

4 extra-large eggs
2 cups milk
1 cup mushrooms
1 tablespoon oil-packed minced garlic
1/2 teaspoon Dijon mustard (optional)
8 ounces sliced bread
Butter for sautéing

Combine the eggs, milk, mushrooms, garlic and Dijon mustard in a blender and process until smooth. Pour into a shallow dish.

Dip the bread in the mushroom mixture, coating both sides. Sauté in butter in a skillet until crisp on the outside and custardy in the center. SERVES 4

OPTION 2: You can tear the bread into pieces and process with the mushroom mixture until smooth. Pack the mixture into buttered muffin cups and bake at 325 degrees for 40 minutes.

OPTION 3: You can prepare the mushroom and bread mixture as for Option 2 and pack it into a loaf pan. Bake at 325 degrees until set. Scoop from the pan to serve like dressing, or remove from the pan and slice to serve.

GERMAN POTATO DUMPLINGS

1 egg yolk
1 cup mashed cooked potatoes
1/3 cup flour
Pinch of salt
1/8 teaspoon pepper
Broth or water

Combine the egg yolk, potatoes, flour, salt and pepper in a bowl and mix to form a soft dough. Roll into balls the diameter of a quarter.

Drop the balls 6 at a time into boiling broth or water in a saucepan. Cook until the dumplings rise to the surface and float.

Remove the dumplings to a bowl and repeat the process until all are cooked. Return the dumplings to the broth, or add to soup or stew. SERVES 4

PEPPERY PEPIN POTATOES

This recipe grew out of one that I attribute originally to the great Jacques Pepin. If he and Julia don't have to agree on everything, then why should we?!? Recipes are merely workable suggestions. Feel free to modify and improve mine and take ALL the credit!

1 (1-pound) package frozen shredded potatoes
1 1/2 cups whole milk, 2% milk or skim milk (your choice will affect the
    richness, but the bouillon cube lends a buttery flavor)
1 chicken bouillon cube
1/2 teaspoon pepper

Place the shredded potatoes in a saucepan and add the milk, chicken bouillon cube and pepper. Mix well.

Simmer over medium heat until most of the milk has been absorbed. SERVES 4

For Western-Style Potatoes, stir chopped onions and peppers in with the potatoes and top with shredded Cheddar cheese to serve.

OVEN-BRONZED VEGETABLES

2 tablespoons extra-virgin olive oil
2 tablespoons Dijon mustard
1/2 teaspoon oil-packed minced garlic
1/2 teaspoon salt
1/4 teaspoon white pepper
3 pounds vegetables such as carrots, potatoes,
    small onions and/or thick asparagus spears

Combine the olive oil, Dijon mustard, garlic, salt and white pepper in a large mixing bowl and mix well.

Peel and trim the vegetables. Cut them into serving pieces, cutting carrots into halves and potatoes into quarters. Add the vegetables to the mixing bowl and toss to coat well.

Arrange the vegetables in a baking dish that will double as a serving dish. Bake at 325 degrees for 45 minutes. Serve from the baking dish. SERVES 8

PAN-PACIFIC NOODLE SALAD

Ramen noodle soup mix is something a lazy cook should never be without!

4 cups salad greens
Chopped scallions, bok choy and carrots
Orange sections, bean sprouts, pea pods, mushrooms (optional)
Noodles from 1 package ramen noodles
Juice of 1 large orange
1/2 cup rice vinegar
1/4 cup extra-virgin olive oil (Meyer lemon olive oil would be fabulous)
1 tablespoon soy sauce
1/4 teaspoon oil-packed minced garlic or shallots
1/4 teaspoon ground ginger
Seasoning packet from the noodles

Combine the salad greens with scallions, bok choy and carrots in a large salad bowl. Add orange sections or other vegetables of choice. Crumble the ramen noodles into the salad.

Combine the orange juice, vinegar, olive oil and soy sauce in a jar with a tight-fitting lid. Add the garlic, ginger and contents of the seasoning packet from the ramen noodles. Shake to blend well. Pour the dressing over the salad and serve immediately. SERVES 4

VEGETABLE COUSCOUS

If you have three or more cups of couscous left over, you can add 1/2 cup of white vinegar and 1/2 cup of orange juice to turn it into a salad!

2 tablespoons oil-packed minced garlic
2 carrots, peeled and sliced
2 zucchini, sliced
2 ribs celery, sliced
1 onion, chopped
1 red bell pepper, chopped
2 vegetable bouillon cubes
1 cup raisins (optional)
1/2 teaspoon cinnamon (optional)
1/2 teaspoon pepper
4 cups water
2 cups uncooked couscous

Sauté the garlic in a large saucepan until warm. Add the carrots, zucchini, celery, onion and red bell pepper. Increase the heat and sauté the vegetables for 3 minutes.

Stir the bouillon cubes, raisins, cinnamon, pepper and water into the saucepan. Bring to a rolling boil.

Stir in the couscous and remove from the heat; cover. Let stand for 20 minutes, stirring well after 10 minutes. SERVES 8 TO 10

NOTE: With the addition of the optional ingredients, this is more aromatic than savory. If you are serving it to "meat-and-potato" people, you might leave out the raisins and cinnamon. If you are going for the whole Middle Eastern feel, serve it with roast leg of lamb and pita bread. GO FOR IT!!

JEWEL BOX RICE

1 large sweet potato
1 medium onion, or 4 to 6 ounces frozen chopped onion
1 red bell pepper
4 cups water
3 chicken bouillon cubes, or 1 tablespoon instant chicken bouillon granules
Pinch of cinnamon
1 cup Uncle Ben's converted rice (must use this type of rice)
1 or 2 cups frozen green peas
1/2 cup raisins

Peel the sweet potato and cut into 1/2-inch pieces. Julienne, chop or slice the onion. Chop the red bell pepper, discarding the stem and seeds.

Bring the water and chicken bouillon cubes to a boil in a 3-quart saucepan. Add the sweet potato, onion, bell pepper, cinnamon and rice.

Bring to a boil and boil over high heat for 5 minutes. Reduce the heat to low and cover the saucepan. Set the timer for 20 minutes and go have a cup of coffee or tea and read a magazine.

Add the green peas and raisins and stir several times. Turn off the burner and let the rice stand, covered, for 5 minutes longer. SERVES 4 TO 6

NOTE: You can add corn, mushrooms, chopped snow peas, etc., to this recipe. It can go in a variety of directions with different additives and different seasonings. In Poland, they do rice like this with white potato, scrambled egg, and green onions, scented with a touch of thyme. It's really great with chicken.

FAUX LEMON GRASS RICE

Faux Lemon Grass Rice is a lovely accompaniment to seafood or anything Asian.

1 cup chopped onion
1/2 teaspoon turmeric
1/2 cup lemon oil (from specialty stores), or safflower oil with lemon zest
3 cups uncooked rice
6 cups water
3 green onions, chopped
Scant pinch of white pepper

Sauté the onion and turmeric in the lemon oil in a saucepan. Add the rice and sauté for 5 minutes longer. Stir in the water and cook for 20 minutes or until the rice is tender. Stir in the green onions and white pepper. SERVES 8 TO 10

FOR THE RELUCTANT CONVERT OR REAL KITCHEN-PHOBIC

IS THIS REALLY A BETTER WAY?
BASIC TRUTHS—HOW TO RE-THINK YOUR APPROACH

Be FEARLESS; it's only food. Nothing is required for you to be fearless but a change in view—a shift—that, starting today, results in a revised course of action. Small changes in the way you think or make choices will result in the slow, steady, very pleasurable process toward mastery. These different choices or efforts will allow you to reap more of the happiness present in a conscious everyday life. Be present!!! Some examples from a frustrated philosophy major…

- Never underestimate the power of homemade soup…love eases all pain…so ladle it up…and listen!

- Entertaining in ways that reveal your true self (whether that's over the top or minimalistic) is creating intimacy—embrace your originality—self-expression isn't just for teenagers!!

- Praise yourself regularly for actively seeking comfort or closeness *with* your sustenance—aren't you smart?

- Anything with apples and cinnamon on the stove or in the oven is definitely aromatherapy—happy people are clearly healthier.

- Cultivate the ability to appreciate everything good in life—and then figure out what is the most important…and how to get more of it.

- Think of your imagination as a muscle—it needs exercise, stimulation, and nourishment, or it will wither away and die.

- Life is meant to be a banquet—not an obligation. Never underestimate the power you have to change yourself FOR THE BETTER...do it!

- Anticipating great results can yield great results—be an optimist in the kitchen and out—accentuate the positive!

- It is how you choose to execute the tasks of your life that determines whether your life will be rich or dull, fulfilling or empty. Don't blame circumstances—change them. What do you want to surround you?

- The oppression created by responsibility is a mindset—take it on—but don't let it make you MISERABLE.

- Criticism can only adversely affect you if you accept it as true, thereby giving it the weight it needs to knock the wind out of you. Do not empower those you don't respect.

Whenever I think I am exhausted, I try to determine if I were to receive a phone call informing me that I had just won the lottery, could I jump onto the roof of my car and dance a jig? YES!

So, is it then my mind and my spirit that ARE exhausted, not my body? Recharge yourself however you can...then persevere.

WHAT IF I NEED TO SUBSTITUTE?

What if you can't find an ingredient, or you don't like it? Or just don't have it on hand? Feel free to substitute!! Only one logical caution—start with a lot less than you think you need—judge the impact, then decide how much more to add...a little at a time. You can always add more, but once it is "in there," it's a lot harder to get it out or mask the heavy-handedness evident in its presence.

Yes, you can make a pot roast without a bay leaf—try a teaspoon of thyme. When deciding on a substitute ingredient, ask yourself what the original ingredient does in the recipe. *Example:* soy sauce adds complexity, salt, and caramel color. Which properties are important (in your opinion) to its taste? Now, without it, is it fine? Or bland? That personal assessment will help you proceed better than any instructions I can give you.

When a recipe calls for anise, you could consider a little five-spice powder, ground fennel, Pernod liqueur, or tarragon, all of which have a licorice taste. If you don't like that flavor, consider any other appropriate aromatic spice. If it is a cookie recipe, cinnamon, cardamon, allspice, and ginger are options—all of which have distinctive smells announcing exactly the flavor they will impart to the cookie instead of anise. So, sniff and go. Your skill will evolve with every effort.

Taste it! Add salt to the soup. Put a bed of spicy sautéed cabbage shreds under the fish, put a dollop of salsa on the underseasoned chicken, dip half of that boring oatmeal cookie in a melted Hershey's candy bar and let it sit! There is always a right answer.

When I make a salad dressing I don't like or a marinade that has one dominating ingredient, my favorite additive is a couple of teaspoons of ground-up whole fresh orange—washed and pitted. Put skin and all into the food processor. Pulse it into a mealy consistency, and add it a teaspoon at a time until you think it's right! It can do WONDERS.

PROBLEM SOLVING:
WHAT IF MY RESULT IS FATTY OR SALTY?

Too much fat floating on the surface? Wrap an ice cube in a paper towel. Blot up the fat quickly and toss it. Repeat as necessary. If it is a flat layer, laying a paper towel over it, then peeling it off works, too.

It tastes too salty! In soups or stews, add three thick potato slices to the over-salted product. Simmer them in it until the potato is clear enough to be done and remove it. You may want to add a little more liquid to compensate for what was lost in the extra cooking. This will also help reduce the saltiness of any product or recipe by expanding its volume while the salt remains the same. For salad dressing that is too salty, add more of the base ingredients to stretch out the salt.

Fish too fishy? Add a few teaspoons of water mixed with white vinegar.

Tomato sauce too sour/acidic? Add fresh lemon juice balanced with a bit of sugar, or just a little sugar to mellow it out.

Salad dressing too bland? Add a little acid like lemon juice with sugar.

Cheese or potato dishes too salty? Add half-and-half or heavy cream a little at a time. It will quickly dilute the salt.

A WORD ABOUT THICKENERS

What if the soup or sauce is too thin? Always dissolve dry THICKENING AGENTS in a small amount of room temperature liquid, then stir the solution into the recipe. This will help to avoid its lumping up in the hot liquid. Keep stirring the thickening product after you add it so it doesn't cluster and lump up anyway.

Properties of Thickener Options:

Flour—can make things a little pasty if you use a lot. If you are making a cream soup, gravy, or sauce, use flour moistened in a "slurry" of water, milk, or cream, or even tinned stock, tomato juice, or wine.

Brown rice flour—silkier, but you can taste it in mild food—it imparts a nuttiness or toasted taste you may or may not like.

Cornstarch—clearer than flour, but as the thickened item sits, it will have a tendency to become gelatinous—like Jell-O; sometimes this is OK, sometimes not.

Arrowroot—my favorite: clear, flavorless, no creaminess, tends to lose its ability to "hold" after refrigeration in liquids but perfect for a little tightening up in stir-frys.

Wondra flour—less likely to lump when heated than regular flour, easier to handle by far.

Mashed potato flakes—great for thickening soups or gravy. Start slowly; you can always add more. Easy to control.

Egg yolks—for richer sauces, beat them in with a wire whip while heating, continue to heat until steaming or at a low rolling boil.

APPLICATIONS:

For Chinese food, use cornstarch or arrowroot moistened in water or sake.

For a vegetable or bean soup, I like potato flakes, but anything will work fine.

To make a really rich sauce that will hold butter in suspension and stretch meager drippings, use egg yolks with a little stock and a melted stick of butter. This makes a Hollandaise-like sauce.

SHOPPING FOR SPECIAL INGREDIENTS, TABLEWARE AND INSPIRATION

Many times, the best places to find exactly the right thing may not be the first places you think of. Marshalls, T.J. Maxx, and Homegoods stores have excellent imported food and beautiful tableware. On a recent trip, I bought pear balsamic vinegar, Meyer lemon olive oil, espresso beans from Italy, marinated mushrooms, Sicilian tomato sauce, Indonesian organic tea, and a half dozen interesting spice blends and salt rubs, as well as mango hot sauce and rum jerk Jamaican barbecue sauce. All of these items will make me want to cook something! Remember, these inventories will vary greatly, so buy items you want when you see them, and don't plan on finding them there again. If you love something, keep track of the name of the importer or manufacturer. You can usually find it that way.

These stores also have various options in china and serving pieces from Irish crystal to English pottery, and they are all deeply discounted from normal retail or even sale prices. Have fun with it. Ross-Simons stores, Williams–Sonoma, Crate and Barrel, Pier One, even Wal-Mart, Costco, and Target, can surprise you, so be alert for more than just what you're looking for! NOTE: This will drive some spouses crazy—you're on a treasure hunt!!! If they don't understand—GO ALONE!

Regionally, we all have wonderful magazines whose sole purpose is to help us consider the possibilities. In Atlanta, every issue of *Atlanta Homes and Lifestyles* displays hundreds of ideas for menus, seasonal tabletops, patio looks, mood lighting, different kinds of parties, and even revolutionary new products particularly in sync with life in the new urban south.

Nationally, *Architectural Digest* has never failed to motivate me to reinvent myself for every new season. JUST WHEN I THINK I CANNOT COOK ANOTHER Thanksgiving dinner...I find I can't wait to plan the menu!!! My indifference is melted by mouthwatering descriptions and beautiful photography. *Bon Appétit*, *Saveur, Cooking Light, Gourmet*, and *Cooks* are all consistently excellent and bound to help you in creating a style all your own.

A STORY ABOUT YOUR OWN RULES

FACT: What we have been taught to believe is true about the kitchen can inhibit us unmercifully.

As a new wife, I enjoyed revealing the natural "talents" I described earlier. This led my husband to want to bring people home for dinner. We had no furniture in our studio in Chicago, so we "set the floor" and "made Chinese" with a fat little Buddha and a few bamboo placemats from Pier One and, of course,…a lot of candles.

I took a borrowed sukiyaki recipe and turned my three-quart Dutch oven into a "wok." Guests offered to bring the sake, so I bought four matching tiny porcelain one-ounce cups for 49 cents each, and presto…I had my first theme party!

If I had known my neighbors at this time, they would have implored me <u>not</u> to do this! You do not invite people over without music, or a TV, or even a place to sit…NEVER. But no one was there to tell me no…my floor was lovely, and the sukiyaki wasn't bad either. Just like that, the young and the clueless had new friends!

During this same period, we started to try wine to go "with" other food. The problem was that the stuff in the 99-cent bin did not taste like the bordeaux at my parents' home. It lacked any fruit or even modest sweetness—it tasted like alcohol and flat peroxide! So, what do you do?…you add the absent characteristics, of course—a little unsweetened raspberry Kool-Aid for fruit and just enough sugar to make it palatable. So, for less than $1.10, I had a bottle of my own beautifully rosy "Raspberry Wine." My guests loved it! I experimented with other additives, mostly successful, and had so much fun!

Then I told my dad, who knew a lot about wine, what I was doing. "You can't do that!!!" he said. "It isn't wine anymore; you're wasting it!" "Buy something you can drink." "That is ridiculous." "People will laugh at you!" Here is the key...because I was already succeeding wildly with "my way," I could dismiss his disdain and proceed. But what may have happened if I had asked him his opinion of the plan before I tried it? This is a very different matter. Doubt might have crept in; I could have lost my nerve.

Now, thirty years later, we have "Blackberry Vines" or "Strawberry Hill" fortified wines with pear, apple, apricot, or even pineapple selling off the shelves. People love these beautifully packaged "new wines." So...it wasn't so ridiculous after all, was it? If my dad had been more open-minded, he could have led the industry with this idea thirty years ago. Go figure. Listen politely, then follow your own heart. Stretch outside your comfort zone regularly. It gets easier every time!

If someone were to take any one of us up on a very high bridge and throw us off with a bungee cord attached to our ankles, the first time might be really scary, and we might HATE it. But, if we were not hurt, by the thirtieth time, we would be getting bored, even if we still didn't like it. The only thing that changed between terror and boredom was what we thought...what we were actually experiencing literally was exactly the same thing.

TIP: *If you want to serve good wine and you don't know a single thing—buy anything produced by Robert Mondavi. You can't go wrong.*

REASONS FOR USING SOURCES

The source list here can be very useful to cooks at every skill level. If you can't do ANYTHING, you can sprinkle meat or fish with a blended rub you think "sounds good." Someone else has made all the balance decisions, and you only have to decide how much to put on. Microwave a vegetable, or make a salad (or buy one), and add bread. You have a meal worthy of a decent restaurant in about twenty minutes. If you start with good ingredients, you are fifty percent of the way done!

Call the 800 numbers listed here, and order catalogs from several. Then, order a few things that spark your imagination or whet your appetite. Keep a record of what you did with it and what to maybe do next time to make it even better. Now you're cooking!

If you are a reader who has been cooking for years, you really need access to new ingredients even more than new cooks. You are probably in a RUTT!!!! If you like curry, try vindaloo on the chicken, add a can of pineapple juice to the iced tea, pour a tin of coconut water into the pot when you make the rice, and sauté the green beans with sweet red pepper and onion instead of boiling them in water. What a totally different experience for almost exactly the same effort.

Expect resistance…"Why did you do that?" "I like the *old* chicken"…etc., etc. Do not be defeated. I once boiled a chicken in a gallon of orange juice on a campfire because I was tired of carrying it! It was really good…and probably the inspiration for my shrimp marinade twenty years later. Use your common sense if it sounds good to you. You'll probably like it!

Today, most grocery stores have widely variable and vastly superior products. Tapenade, marinated artichoke hearts, buffalo mozzarella, pickled mushrooms, great bread and Gorgonzola picked up at the local chain store is a simple cocktail party in a bag! Buy what looks good to you, anytime. Even if you have the best availability in the world in your area, specialty purveyors are PASSIONATE; their focus and enthusiasm can transport your own ideas to a whole new level of consideration. Don't miss the opportunity to be exposed to that. It still gets me so motivated to find fabulous new products. I want to do another book just to match up exceptional ingredients with recipes and sample menus! Happy hunting!

ACKNOWLEDGMENTS

Thanks to my mom and dad, Ruth and Russell Kliem, for letting me enjoy an amazing variety of excellent food prepared at their hands and take it for granted. The joyful results of their efforts made me want to cook, just to share something wonderful with the people I love.

Thanks to Jordan Benefield, my gifted daughter, for her cheerful editorial encouragement.

To my boys, Trent and Reid, thanks for being the world's most enthusiastic eaters. It made me find the fast ways to dinner when I was too tired to pick up Chinese.

For twenty years of exemplary lessons of what style is...and what it isn't, thanks to *Architectural Digest*.

A big gracias to Texas Girl and confidante Susan Glahn, who didn't let me get overwhelmed and always provided invaluable collaboration, especially on the Killer Frozen Margarita recipe.

To my staff at the Metropolitan Club, most especially Lara Storm and Mark Simpson, thanks for giving me the time it took to write this book.

For convincing me I should write a book and for the invaluable guidance that followed, thanks to my friend Gina Christman.

Thanks to Amber Goodwin, Jean Froehlich, Debra Peterson, and Shana Kaufman, who suffered through my handwriting and wrestled it into recipes, again and again.

A thank-you beyond words goes to my clients, who have become my friends; they discovered my strengths early on and gave me the opportunities to develop style and technique. These were the most important occasions of their lives, and I will be forever grateful they chose to share those times with me.

Thanks to my friends Dee and Susan at Favorite Recipes® Press for not giving up on me.

And most of all, to my dear husband, Chad, who, through his pure delight, gave me the gift of believing in myself...in the kitchen and out.

CLOSING

How do you think it is possible for us to be intimidated by something everyone in the world has done two or three times a day since the beginning of time? Well, let's look at food from a historical perspective for a minute: Until the last several hundred years or so, eating *could* be a pleasure, but it was largely linked to survival. Eating was much more about what you *could* get, rather than what you might want. So, regular folks who were creative enough to turn shoe leather into something edible were "gifted," absolutely.

Today, the products we start with, when assembled alertly, are already PERFECT! So, we do not need to be even remotely competent in the kitchen to get very wonderful results. Two hundred years ago, salt was currency. The only product that could stabilize food without refrigeration was strictly controlled and expensive. Today, you have as much salt, fresh herbs, prime meat, great wine, luscious oils, just-picked fruit and vegetables as your pocketbook can handle. So, how could this be hard?

Currently, chefs are celebrities. So, in a lot of cases, it's their job and the job of publicists and public relations teams to convince you to just eat out and revel in their brilliance. Okay—that can be fun. But it also leads us to believe only the thirty-ingredient barbecue sauce—lacquered onto free-range chicken by a team of three chefs—at great personal expense—is really great food. A thirty-ingredient sauce is just silly. So, unless you are a frustrated chemist or mad scientist....don't even try it.

In the days of Escoffier and Brillat-Savarin, there were no convenience foods. To make a lobster bisque, you hammered the empty shells, sautéed them with paprika and butter to nudge some bit of toasty "lobsterness" from their reluctant remains, then boiled that in a gallon of water for six hours, strained the shell out, and then reduced the gallon to a quart or a pint of lobster stock. Now, in our modern world, someone else does it for you and puts the essence with a little salt in a lobster base—like a chicken bouillon cube, only lobster. So, in a restaurant where thirty lobsters are served and the shells remain useful, this elaborate exercise has merit; but, in your kitchen for two, four, or six, it is a TORTUROUS effort...especially for someone who prefers eating to cooking.

That is the essence of this book—the greatest result with the LEAST amount of effort...less preparation, less shopping, less planning, and less cleanup. More time to enjoy eating and spending time together!

Believe it or not, almost every aspect of the food world has a "lunatic fringe." People who work in these fields are very focused, excited, and usually very well informed about cheese, wine, heirloom vegetables, game, exotic meats, china, hot sauce, regional ingredients, cookware, cookbooks, you name it. You can find people who live their lives around it. Expose yourself to these...purveyors of "PASSION." Seek them out, let them overwhelm you with information, and save from it what is meaningful to you. Any one of these areas of interest could provide the inspiration for your next effort; if you can't muster your own enthusiasm, borrow someone else's!

SOURCES

Dean & DeLuca
www.dean-deluca.com
Specialty foods and gourmet spices
800-221-7714

Penzeys Spices
www.penzeys.com
Exotic spices and spice blends
800-741-7787

Adriana's Caravan
www.adrianascaravan.com
Unusual spices and condiments, whole foods, and ingredients
800-316-0820

Bella Cucina
www.bellacucinaartfulfood.com
Artful Italian specialties available at Saks or by Internet or catalog
800-580-5674

Victoria Gourmet
www.vgourmet.com
Seasoning blends
866-972-6879

Duck Trap River Fishfarm
www.ducktrap.com
All manner of smoked seafood
207-338-6280

American Spoon Foods
www.spoon.com
Unusual food and heirloom condiments
800-222-5886

The Mozzarella Co.
www.mozzco.com
Hand-crafted cheeses and cheese products
800-798-2954

Le Saucier
www.drhot.net
More than 500 assorted international specialty food products
617-847-1846

Bickford Flavors
www.bickfordflavors.com
One hundred flavors of extracts
800-283-8322

Legal Seafood
www.legalseafoods.com
Great seafood!
800-328-3474

Cinnabar Specialty Foods
www.cinnabarfoods.com
Exotic condiments and chutneys, even seaweed
415-928-4288

GAZIN'S www.gazins.com	Cajun and Creole products and spice blends	800-262-6410
Timbercrest Farms www.timbercrest.com	Organic and unsulfered dried fruits, nuts, and sun-dried tomatoes	888-374-9325
Northwestern Coffee Mills www.nwcoffeemills.com	Unusual and salt-free spices, ingredients, coffee, and exotic teas	800-243-5283
Napa Style www.napastyle.com	Signature oils, dressings, mustards, flours, grains, spices, and recipes	866-776-6272
Figueroa Brothers Kenner, LA 70062 www.spice-exchange.com	Hot sauces, spice blends, coffees, and marinades	800-886-6354
Numi Oakland, CA 94620 www.numitea.com	Ethnic and unusual tea blends. Try golden chai as a marinade!	510-567-8903
Mountain Fruit Company Chico, CA 95927 No Website	Jarred fruit like you would do yourself—nothing else like it. Try Always Apricot right from the jar.	800-401-9588
El Paso Chile Company El Paso, TX 79901 www.elpasochile.com	Prepared sauces, salsas, and southwestern ingredients	888-472-5727
Pepper Creek Farms Lawton, OK 73505 www.peppercreekfarms.com	Prepared, ready-to-use spoon foods, great honey mustard, dip mixes, and organic bread mixes	866-972-6879

INDEX

SOME ASSEMBLY REQUIRED

BILL TO: SHIP TO:

_____   _____

_____   _____

_____   _____

phone: _____   phone: _____

Number of books _____ @$19.95 = _____   *Shipping Charges:
Over 10 books, deduct 20%   1 book - $3.95
                                                         2 books - $5.00
Tax   7%   _____   3 books - $6.00
                                                         4 books - $7.00
*Shipping   _____   5 books - $8.00
                                                         6-9 books - $9.00
Total charges   _____   10 or more books - $10.00

Inscription/Dedication:

_____

_____

_____

Credit Card Information: Order Line: 404-754-4500
                                            Fax orders to: 678-517-2001
Card Type: _____

Name on Card: _____   Mail to:
                                   Meridian International Publishing
Expiration Date: ____ / ____   Attn: Lu Cross
                                            700 Park Regency Place
Credit Card Number: _____   Suite 1702
                                            Atlanta, GA 30326
Signature: _____